Be Your Own CBT Therapist

Image credits

Teach
Yourself®

Be Your Own CBT Therapist

Windy Dryden

For UK order enquiries: please contact Bookpoint Ltd, 130 Milton
Park, Abingdon, Oxon OX14 4SB. *Telephone*: +44 (0) 1235 827720.
Fax: +44 (0) 1235 400454. Lines are open 0900–1700, Monday to
Saturday, with a 24-hour message answering service. Details about
our titles and how to order are available at www.teachyourself.com

Long renowned as the authoritative source for self-guided
learning – with more than 50 million copies sold worldwide –
the **Teach Yourself** series includes over 500 titles in the fields of
languages, crafts, hobbies, business, computing and education.

British Library Cataloguing in Publication Data: a catalogue record
for this title is available from the British Library.

First published in UK 2011 by Hodder Education, part of
Hachette UK, 338 Euston Road, London NW1 3BH.

The **Teach Yourself** name is a registered trade mark of
Hodder Headline.

Typeset by MPS Limited, a Macmillan Company.

Printed in Great Britain for Hodder Education, an Hachette UK
Company, 338 Euston Road, London NW1 3BH, by CPI Cox &
Wyman, Reading, Berkshire RG1 8EX.

The publisher has used its best endeavours to ensure that the URLs
for external websites referred to in this book are correct and active
at the time of going to press. However, the publisher and the author
have no responsibility for the websites and can make no guarantee
that a site will remain live or that the content will remain relevant,
decent or appropriate.

Hachette UK's policy is to use papers that are natural, renewable
and recyclable products and made from wood grown in sustainable
forests. The logging and manufacturing processes are expected to
conform to the environmental regulations of the country of origin.

Impression number   10 9 8 7 6 5 4 3 2 1
Year   2015 2014 2013 2012 2011

Contents

	Meet the author	vi
	In one minute	vii
	Tables and figures	ix
1	What is Rational Emotive Behaviour Therapy (REBT)? – an introduction	1
2	Understanding the 'Situational ABC' framework	17
3	Tackling your problems: an overview	28
4	Identifying and formulating your problems and goals	40
5	Selecting and working with a target problem and a specific example of that problem	49
6	Using the 'Situational ABC' framework to assess your specific example and to set goals	57
7	Focusing on and questioning your beliefs	73
8	Strengthening your conviction in your rational beliefs	89
9	Responding to highly distorted thoughts at 'C'	100
10	Coming back to 'A'	123
11	Using established and new skills across the board	128
12	Dealing with lapses and preventing relapse	143
13	Maintaining your gains	155
14	Dealing with obstacles to change	163
15	Dealing with anxiety	184
16	Dealing with depression	206
	Taking it further	229
	Appendices	231
	Index	243

Meet the author

Welcome to *Be Your Own CBT Therapist*!

I have been in the helping professions for well over 30 years and I am still passionate about helping people to become emotionally healthy in the face of life's adversities. I have worked with thousands of individuals in my career in a variety of settings and while face-to-face counselling is powerful, I also hold that people can gain much from using books such as this one and work, yes work, to help themselves.

While I can teach you how to think rational thinking and apply it in your everyday life when you encounter life's adversities, only you can learn these principles. For there is a great difference between teaching and learning. As a psychological educator, I have a responsibility to be as clear as possible in outlining how you can think more rationally, but it is down to you to tailor these ideas to suit you and to apply them in your life.

Many years ago I had a bad stammer and was anxious about speaking in public. I used to shy away from speaking to people. Now I can speak in public, often to large audiences, without anxiety! How did I manage this? By putting into practice some of this book's ideas. So, I am not only a well-trained Rational Emotive Behaviour therapist, I have also used REBT in my life and have become more emotionally healthy through the application of rational thinking. If I can do this, so can you!

In one minute

Think rationally, be emotionally healthy!

Rational thinking is thinking that is flexible and non-extreme. It helps you to roll with the punches of life, deal with adversities, regroup and get on with the business of living.

To think rationally, you need to:

▶ recognize what you want, but not demand that you have to get it
▶ evaluate *not* getting what you want as bad, but not awful
▶ tolerate the discomfort of not getting your desires met
▶ accept yourself, others and life along the way.

You have to practise rational thinking for it to take root. Act on it and don't just think it. If you do, you will learn to be emotionally healthy in the face of life's adversities.

Tables and figures

Table 1.1 Unhealthy negative emotions and their healthy
alternatives.   8

Table 1.2 The major behaviours associated with the eight
unhealthy and healthy negative emotions.   11

Table 3.1 Common themes associated with unhealthy negative
emotions.   35

Table 6.1 Unhealthy negative emotions and illustrative
subsequent distorted thinking.   61

Table 6.2 Healthy negative emotions and illustrative subsequent
realistic and balanced thinking.   66

Table 6.3 Irrational beliefs.   68

Table 6.4 Rational beliefs.   69

Table 6.5 Harvey's 'Situational ABC' form without instructions.   70

Table 7.1 Reasons why rigid beliefs are false and illogical and
have largely unhealthy consequences and why flexible beliefs are
true and logical and have largely healthy consequences.   76

Table 7.2 Reasons why awfulizing beliefs are false and
illogical and have largely unhealthy consequences and why
non-awfulizing beliefs are true and logical and have largely
healthy consequences.   80

Table 7.3 Reasons why discomfort intolerance beliefs are false
and illogical and have largely unhealthy consequences and why
discomfort tolerance beliefs are true and logical and have largely
healthy consequences.   82

Table 7.4 Reasons why depreciation beliefs are false and
illogical and have largely unhealthy consequences and why
acceptance beliefs are true and logical and have largely healthy
consequences.   85

Table 9.1 Twelve thinking errors and their realistic and
balanced alternatives.   107

Table 9.2 Descriptions, foundations and illustrations of thinking errors and their realistic and balanced alternatives.   108

Table 12.1 The application of the 'Situational ABC' framework to the identification of a vulnerability factor.   146

Table 12.2 How Freda applied the 'Situational ABC' framework to the identification of her vulnerability factor.   146

Table 15.1 'ABC' formulation of anxiety.   186

Table 15.2 'ABC' formulation of concern.   186

Table 16.1 'ABC' formulation of depression.   207

Table 16.2 'ABC' formulation of sadness.   207

Figure 11.1 How a core irrational belief combines with uncertainty to create a distorted inference at 'A'.   141

Figure 15.1 How holding a core irrational belief influences the inferences we form at 'A' in anxiety.   204

Figure 16.1 How holding a core irrational belief influences the inferences we form at 'A' in depression.   227

1

What is Rational Emotive Behaviour Therapy (REBT)? – an introduction

In this introductory chapter you will learn:
- *what the terms 'rational' and 'irrational' mean in Rational Emotive Behaviour Therapy (REBT)*
- *how REBT conceives of emotion and behaviour*
- *what are the three levels of therapy that REBT addresses and in what preferred order.*

In the field of counselling and psychotherapy today, much attention is being focused on a therapeutic tradition known as Cognitive Behaviour Therapy (which I will refer to as CBT). In my view, CBT is a therapeutic tradition rather than a therapeutic approach because there are, in fact, many approaches that come under the umbrella of CBT. While there are differences among these approaches, they all share the view that our emotional problems are closely linked to how we think about ourselves, others and the world and how we act based on such thinking. All this goes back to the early Stoic philosophers, one of whom, Epictetus, said: 'People are disturbed not by things, but by their views of things.'

One of these CBT approaches is known as Rational Emotive Behaviour Therapy (henceforth called REBT), which is the focus of this book. It is the approach I am going to use to show you how you can think rationally so that you can be emotionally healthy in the face of life's adversities. Thus, while the title highlights the therapeutic tradition this book is based on a specific approach within this tradition.

In this opening chapter I will discuss in turn the four words that comprise the therapy's name...

1 **Rational**
2 **Emotive**
3 **Behaviour and**
4 **Therapy...**

as a way of explaining what REBT is and what its major focus is.

Rational

When Albert Ellis, the famous American clinical psychologist, established the therapy in the 1950s, he called it 'Rational Therapy'. He did so because he wanted to stress that emotional problems are based on irrational thinking and that if we are to address these problems effectively, we need to change such thinking to its rational equivalent. It is interesting to note that, while REBT has had two previous names, the term 'rational' is common to all three names. It is the constant feature that spans REBT's 50-plus years' history. So what do REBT therapists currently mean by the term 'rational'? I can best answer this question if I contrast it with the term 'irrational'.

The terms 'rational' and 'irrational' in current REBT theory are most commonly used as adjectives in front of the noun 'beliefs'. Such beliefs can also be thought of as attitudes in that they describe a person's stance or position towards something.

Let me consider the major characteristics of rational beliefs and contrast these with the major characteristics of irrational beliefs. In what follows, I will consider the rational belief in the left-hand column and the irrational belief in the right-hand column to facilitate the comparison.

A rational belief is flexible or non-extreme	*An irrational belief is rigid or extreme*
1 A rational belief is flexible	**1 An irrational belief is rigid**
Here is an example of a rational belief that is flexible:	Here is an example of an irrational belief that is rigid:
'I want my colleague to like me, but she does not have to do so.'	*'My colleague has to like me.'*
Imagine that you hold such a belief. As you do so, you will see that this belief is flexible	To compare this belief with the flexible version in the left-hand column, we need to state it in its full form:

A rational belief is flexible or non-extreme	An irrational belief is rigid or extreme

because while you assert what you want (i.e. '*I want my colleague to like me…*'), you also acknowledge that you do not have to get what you want (i.e. '*…but she does not have to do so*').

'*I want my colleague to like me, therefore she has to do so.*'

Again, imagine that you hold this belief. As you do so, you will see that this belief is rigid because, while you not only assert what you want (i.e. '*I want my colleague to like me…*'), you also demand that you have to get it (i.e. '*… therefore she has to do so*').

2 A rational belief is non-extreme

Here is an example of a rational belief that is non-extreme:

'*It is bad if my colleague does not like me, but not the end of the world.*'

Again imagine that you hold this belief. As you do so, you will see that this belief is non-extreme because, while you assert that you find the event negative (i.e. '*It is bad if my colleague does not like me…*'), you also acknowledge that such an evaluation is not extreme because it could always be worse (i.e. '*…but not the end of the world*').

2 An irrational belief is extreme

Here is an example of an irrational belief that is extreme:

'*It is the end of the world if my colleague does not like me.*'

To compare it to the non-extreme version in the left-hand column we need to state it in its full form:

'*It is bad if my colleague does not like me, and therefore it is the end of the world.*'

Again imagine that you hold this belief. As you do so you will see that this belief is extreme because you not only assert that you find the event negative (i.e. '*It is bad if my colleague does not like me…*'), you also claim that it could not be worse (i.e. '*…and therefore it is the end of the world*').

(Contd)

Imagine that you hold the following rational belief that I introduced above: '*I want my colleague to like me, but she does not have to do so.*' You will note that this belief is made up of two parts:

▶ '*I want my colleague to like me…*'
▶ '*…but she does not have to do so.*'

Let's take one part at a time. First, you can prove that you would like your colleague to like you; after all this is your desire. Also, you can probably cite reasons why you want your colleague to like you (e.g. it makes for a good working relationship where you can help each other). So, the first part of your belief is true.

Now let's look at the second part of the rational belief. You can also prove that the other person does not have to like you. To state otherwise would be to deny that person free choice.

So if both parts of this rational belief are true then we can say that the belief taken as a whole is true.

Now imagine that you hold the following irrational belief that I introduced above: '*My colleague has to like me.*' Again this belief is made up of two parts:

▶ '*I want my colleague to like me…*'
▶ '*…and therefore she has to do so.*'

Let's take one part at a time. First, you can again prove that you would like the other person to like you for reasons discussed opposite. So, the first part of your belief is true.

Now let's look at the second part of the irrational belief. You cannot prove that your colleague has to like you. If that were true, she would have no choice but to like you. This demanding component of your irrational belief in effect robs your colleague of free choice, which she retains in the face of your demand. Thus, this second part is false.

As both parts of a belief have to be true for the belief to be true then we can say that the irrational belief is false.

Also, when we consider this irrational belief in its short form (i.e. '*My colleague has to like me*'), then it is clear that

A rational belief is true	An irrational belief is false
	it is false since it again attempts to rob your colleague of the freedom not to like you which she does in reality have.

A rational belief is sensible	An irrational belief is not sensible
Taking the rational belief '*I want my colleague to like me, but she does not have to do so*', we can ask the question: does this belief make sense? We can answer that it does since you are explicitly acknowledging that there is no connection between what you want and what you have to get.	Taking the full form of your irrational belief '*I want my colleague to like me, and therefore she has to do so*', we can again ask the question: does this belief make sense? Here our answer is that it does not because it asserts that there is a connection between what you want and what you have to get. The idea that because you want something you have to get it is, in fact, childish nonsense when coming from an adult.

A rational belief is largely constructive	An irrational belief is largely unconstructive
When you hold a rational belief the consequences of doing so will be largely constructive. For example, let's suppose that you hold the rational belief, '*I want my colleague to like me, but she does not have to do so*', and you bring this belief to a situation where your colleague snaps at you for no	When you hold an irrational belief the consequences of doing so will be largely unconstructive. For example, let's suppose that you hold the irrational belief, '*My colleague must like me*', and you bring this belief to the situation where your colleague snaps at you for no good reason.

(Contd)

A rational belief is largely constructive	An irrational belief is largely unconstructive
good reason. In this situation you will experience three different, but related, consequences which I will now illustrate:	In this situation you will experience three different, but related, consequences which I will now illustrate. As I do so, compare these consequences to those that stem from your belief if it were rational (see opposite):
1 **Emotional consequence** Here you will tend to be concerned about your colleague's response, but not anxious about it.	1 **Emotional consequence** Here you will tend to be anxious, rather than concerned, about your colleague's response.
2 **Behavioural consequence** Here you will be likely to enquire of your colleague in an open way if there is anything wrong.	2 **Behavioural consequence** Here you will tend to avoid your colleague or try desperately to get her to like you.
3 **Thinking consequence** Here you will tend to think that your colleague is upset with someone or something which could be to do with you, but may well be nothing to do with you.	3 **Thinking consequence** Here you will tend to think that your colleague is upset with you rather than with someone or something that had nothing to do with you.

Emotive

The term 'emotive' in REBT means that which is relevant to your emotions. Like every other approach to therapy, REBT is based on a model of emotions. Since REBT is a therapeutic approach it is primarily concerned with relieving people's emotional disturbance. However, it also acknowledges that people are bound to have negative emotions when faced with negative life events (henceforth called adversities in this book). To accommodate these two positions REBT distinguishes between emotions that are negative in tone and have largely unconstructive consequences and emotions that are negative in tone and have largely constructive consequences. The former are known as unhealthy negative emotions (UNEs) and the latter healthy negative emotions (HNEs).

THE REBT MODEL OF EMOTIONS

Insight

People are not disturbed by the adversities they face; rather, they disturb themselves about these adversities by the rigid and extreme beliefs that they hold about them.

The REBT model of emotion states that the emotions that we experience are based largely on the beliefs that we hold about ourselves, others and the world. More specifically it states that our unhealthy negative emotions about life's adversities are based largely on the irrational beliefs that we hold about these adversities and that, if we want to experience healthy negative emotions about the adversities in question, we need to change our irrational beliefs to rational beliefs.

This is shown in the model below in which 'A' stands for adversity, 'B' for beliefs and 'C' for the consequences of these beliefs (in this case the *emotional* consequences). This is REBT's famous 'ABC' model which I will discuss in greater detail in Chapter 2.

A	B	C
Adversity	Irrational beliefs	Unhealthy negative emotions
Adversity	Rational beliefs	Healthy negative emotions

Let me illustrate this model by referring to the example that I introduced earlier in this chapter:

A	B	C
Adversity ▶ *'My colleague may not like me.'*	Irrational belief ▶ *'My colleague must like me.'*	Unhealthy negative emotion ▶ *Anxiety*
Adversity ▶ *'My colleague may not like me.'*	Rational belief ▶ *'I want my colleague to like me, but she does not have to do so.'*	Healthy negative emotion ▶ *Concern*

I will discuss how you can deal with the problematic emotions of anxiety and depression in Chapters 15 and 16 when you encounter some of life's adversities. Because these adversities are negative, it is not appropriate for you to feel good about them or even neutral about them. It is healthy to experience negative emotions, but not problematic ones, about such life events. These problematic emotions in REBT are unhealthy negative emotions (UNEs) and these are listed in Table 1.1 and contrasted with their healthy negative equivalents (HNEs).

Table 1.1 Unhealthy negative emotions and their healthy alternatives.

Unhealthy negative emotions	Healthy negative emotions[1]
Anxiety	Concern
Depression	Sadness
Guilt	Remorse
Shame	Disappointment
Hurt	Sorrow
Unhealthy anger	Healthy anger
Unhealthy jealousy	Healthy jealousy
Unhealthy envy	Healthy envy

[1] We do not have commonly agreed words in the English language to describe healthy negative emotions. The terms that I have used in the right-hand column of the above table are my own. Feel free to use alternative terms that are more meaningful to you.

Insight
Unhealthy negative emotions (UNEs) largely stem from irrational beliefs about life's adversities while healthy negative emotions (HNEs) stem largely from rational beliefs about these same adversities.

INTELLECTUAL V EMOTIVE UNDERSTANDING

The other major area where the term 'emotive' comes up in REBT is in distinguishing between two different types of understanding: intellectual understanding and emotive understanding. These are particularly important when a person is trying to change an irrational belief to its rational belief alternative.

Let me illustrate this distinction by using the above example where you currently hold the irrational belief (i.e. 'My colleague must like me') and your colleague has snapped at you. Let's suppose that you acknowledge that your irrational belief is irrational (meaning that it is rigid, false, not sensible and largely unconstructive – see above). And let's assume, furthermore, that you acknowledge that your rational alternative belief (i.e. 'I want my colleague to like me, but she does not have to do so') is rational (meaning that it is flexible, true, sensible and largely constructive).

When your understanding of these two points is *intellectual* in nature, you say things like 'Well, I can understand this in my head, but not in my heart' and 'I understand it, but I don't feel it'. Here, you will still feel anxious about the prospect of your colleague not liking you, you will act in ways that are consistent with your irrational belief (i.e. you will either avoid your colleague or desperately try to get her to like you) and you will tend to think in highly distorted ways about your colleague (e.g. 'She is definitely upset with me' and 'If I don't win her over immediately, she will never like me again'). In other words, while you understand intellectually the reason why your irrational belief is irrational and why your rational belief is rational, this understanding has little or no impact on your emotions, behaviour and subsequent thinking. You still think, act and feel in ways consistent with your irrational belief even though you know it is irrational.

However, when your understanding of these points is *emotive* in nature, you not only grasp the points intellectually, but you also feel, think and act in ways that are consistent with the rational belief and that are inconsistent with the irrational belief. Thus, you will feel concerned, but not anxious, about the prospect of your colleague not liking you, you will act in ways that are consistent with your rational belief (i.e. you will check out with her why she snapped at you) and you will tend to think in realistic ways about your colleague (e.g. 'She may or may not be upset with me' and 'If she is upset with me, we can talk it through and resolve the issue'). In other words, you understand the reason why your irrational belief is irrational and why your rational belief is rational, and this understanding has a decided constructive impact on your emotions, behaviour and subsequent thinking. You think, act and feel in ways consistent with your rational belief.

In REBT, we argue that intellectual understanding is a necessary but insufficient ingredient for constructive psychological change and many of the chapters in this book are devoted to helping you to move from such intellectual understanding to the emotive understanding necessary for such change to occur.

> **Insight**
> Understanding intellectually that your beliefs are irrational is an important first step, but it isn't sufficient to change them. To do this, you need to truly see that your beliefs are irrational and you need to feel, think and act in ways that are consistent with your rational belief alternatives.

Behaviour

The term 'behaviour' in REBT refers to both overt behaviour and to an urge to act that is not translated into overt behaviour. The latter is known as an action tendency. REBT's model of behaviour parallels its model of emotions in arguing that irrational beliefs tend to lead to behaviour that is largely unconstructive in effect and that rational beliefs lead to behaviour that is largely constructive in effect. The former is associated with unhealthy negative emotions (UNEs) and the latter with healthy negative emotions (HNEs).

This is shown in the following model in which 'A' stands for adversity, 'B' for beliefs and 'C' for the consequences of these beliefs (in this case the *behavioural* consequences).

A	B	C
Adversity	Irrational beliefs	Unconstructive behaviour
Adversity	Rational beliefs	Constructive behaviour

Let me illustrate this model by referring again to the example that I introduced earlier in this chapter.

A	B	C
Adversity	Irrational belief	Unconstructive behaviour
▸ *'My colleague may not like me.'*	▸ *'My colleague must like me.'*	▸ *Avoidance of colleague* ▸ *Desperate attempts to get colleague to like me*

A	B	C
Adversity	Rational belief	Constructive behaviour
▶ 'My colleague may not like me.'	▶ 'I want my colleague to like me, but she does not have to do so.'	▶ Asking colleague directly if there is anything wrong

In Table 1.2 I outline the major behaviours associated with the eight unhealthy and healthy negative emotions listed above.

Table 1.2 The major behaviours associated with the eight unhealthy and healthy negative emotions.

Unhealthy negative emotion with associated unconstructive behaviours and action tendencies	Healthy negative emotion with associated constructive behaviours and action tendencies
Anxiety ▶ Withdrawing from threat ▶ Avoiding threat ▶ Seeking reassurance even though not reassurable ▶ Seeking safety from threat	**Concern** ▶ Confronting threat ▶ Seeking reassurance when reassurable
Depression ▶ Prolonged withdrawal from enjoyable activities	**Sadness** ▶ Engaging with enjoyable activities after a period of mourning or adjustment to the loss
Guilt ▶ Begging for forgiveness	**Remorse** ▶ Asking, not begging, for forgiveness
Shame ▶ Withdrawing from others ▶ Avoiding eye contact with others	**Disappointment** ▶ Keeping in contact with others ▶ Maintaining eye contact with others

(Contd)

Unhealthy negative emotion with associated unconstructive behaviours and action tendencies	Healthy negative emotion with associated constructive behaviours and action tendencies
Hurt ▶ Sulking	**Sorrow** ▶ Assertion and communicating with others
Unhealthy anger ▶ Aggression (direct and indirect)	**Healthy anger** ▶ Assertion
Unhealthy jealousy ▶ Prolonged suspicious questioning of the other person ▶ Checking on the other ▶ Restricting the other	**Healthy jealousy** ▶ Brief, open-minded questioning of the other person ▶ Not checking on the other ▶ Not restricting the other
Unhealthy envy ▶ Spoiling the other's enjoyment of the desired possession	**Healthy envy** ▶ Striving to gain a similar possession for oneself if it is truly what you want

The behaviours listed in Table 1.2 are what a person does or tends to do when her irrational or rational belief about an adversity has been fully activated. However, the impact of belief on behaviour can be seen in other ways.

SHORT-TERM SELF-PROTECTIVE BEHAVIOUR

In the 'ABC' model that I have presented in this chapter, an adversity occurs or is deemed to occur at 'A', the person holds a belief about this adversity at 'B' and experiences emotional, behavioural and thinking consequences of holding this belief at 'C'. In this model the person's belief (e.g. 'My colleague must like me') is specific to the specific adversity that she encounters.

However, beliefs can be held at a more general level (e.g. 'People with whom I work must like me') and, when a belief is more general in nature, the person has a tendency to bring such a belief with them, as it were, to situations where a relevant adversity may occur.

Thus, in our example, if a person holds a general irrational belief (e.g. 'People with whom I work must like me'), then the person will be hypersensitive to the possibility of not being liked by a colleague and act to prevent this adversity actually occurring (e.g. by being extra nice to a person whom she thinks may show, but has not yet shown, some disapproval of her). In this way the person is acting to protect herself in the short-term, but the longer-term effect of this behaviour is unconstructive in a number of ways:

▶ she does not get to test out her hunch that the person will disapprove of her
▶ she does not get to deal constructively with such disapproval should it occur and
▶ she tends to maintain her irrational belief since she is acting in a way that is consistent with it.

OVERCOMPENSATORY BEHAVIOUR

When a person holds an irrational belief and particularly one that is general in nature, then she may try to deal with actual or potential adversities by behaving in a manner that is overcompensatory. By using overcompensatory behaviour the person is trying to prove to herself the opposite of what she actually thinks is the truth about her, the other person or the world. A common example of this occurs when a person privately considers that he would be weak if he can't deal with a challenge, but tries to prove to himself that he is strong by facing an even greater challenge.

Therapy

The word 'therapy' comes from the Greek *therapeia* meaning 'a service, an attendance' which, in turn, is related to the Greek verb *therapeuo* meaning 'I wait upon'.

REBT therapists, therefore, can be seen to offer a 'service' to people who have problems in a number of areas:

1 emotional problems;
2 practical, dissatisfaction problems *and*
3 personal development problems.

A distinctive feature of REBT is that it outlines a logical order for dealing with these problems.

DISTURBANCE BEFORE DISSATISFACTION

REBT argues that, unless there are good reasons to the contrary, it is best for us to address our emotional problems before our dissatisfaction problems. The reasoning is as follows. If we try and deal with our dissatisfaction before we deal with our emotional disturbance, then our disturbed feelings will get in the way of our efforts to change directly the adversities about which we are dissatisfied.

For example, let's take the case of Paul who is dissatisfied about his wife's spending habits. However, he is also unhealthily angry about her behaviour and every time he talks to her about it he makes himself angry about it, raises his voice to his wife and makes pejorative remarks about her and her spending behaviour. Now what is the likely impact of Paul's expression of unhealthy anger on his wife? Does it encourage her to stand back and look objectively at her own behaviour? Of course it doesn't. Paul's angry behaviour is more likely to lead his wife to become unhealthily angry herself and/or to become defensive. In Paul's case, his anger had, in fact, both effects on his wife.

Now, let's suppose that Paul first addressed his unhealthy anger and then discussed his dissatisfaction with his wife. His annoyance at her behaviour, but his acceptance of her as a person, would help him to view her own behaviour perhaps as a sign of emotional disturbance and his compassion for her would have very different effects on her. She would probably be less defensive and, because Paul would not be unhealthily angry, then his wife would also be less likely to be unhealthily angry. With anger out of the picture, the stage would be set for Paul to address the reasons for his dissatisfaction more effectively.

DISTURBANCE BEFORE DEVELOPMENT

In the late 1960s and early 1970s I used to go to a number of encounter groups. This was the era of personal growth or development. However, there were a number of casualties of these groups and when these occurred it was because attendees were preoccupied with issues of emotional disturbance and they were being pushed too hard to go into areas of development that warranted greater resilience.

In general, then, it is very difficult for us to develop ourselves when we are emotionally disturbed. To focus on areas of development when someone is emotionally disturbed is akin to encouraging that person to climb a very steep hill with very heavy weights attached to their ankles. First help the person to remove their ankle weights (i.e. address their emotional disturbance) before discussing the best way of climbing the hill!

DISSATISFACTION BEFORE DEVELOPMENT

Abraham Maslow (1968) is perhaps best known for his work on self-actualization. The relevance of this concept for our present discussion is this. It is very difficult for humans to focus on higher-order 'needs' when we are preoccupied with issues with respect to lower-order needs. Thus, if a person is faced with a general dissatisfying life experience which cannot be compartmentalized and also wants to explore his writing ambitions, he should address the former first – unless this life dissatisfaction will help him write a better book!

Insight

If you are disturbed about a dissatisfaction, address your disturbance before you address the dissatisfaction. When you have addressed the dissatisfaction, you are in the best frame of mind to develop yourself.

I have outlined REBT's preferred order in dealing with problems; it also values flexibility. Thus, if a person wants to deal with his problems in a different order, he should do so and observe the results. If it works, that is fine. If not, then REBT's preferred position may prove to yield better results. The proof of the pudding is in the eating!

Now that I have discussed the four terms that make up the name of the therapy, in the next chapter I will consider REBT's famous ABC model in much greater detail.

THINGS TO REMEMBER

▶ Rational beliefs are flexible or non-extreme, true, sensible and largely constructive.

▶ Irrational beliefs are rigid or extreme, false, not sensible and largely unconstructive.

▶ Our beliefs about life's adversities have a profound effect on our emotional and behavioural response to them.

▶ When we hold rational beliefs about adversities our emotions will be negative and healthy and our behaviour will be largely constructive.

▶ When we hold irrational beliefs about adversities our emotions will be negative and unhealthy and our behaviour will be largely unconstructive.

▶ To change irrational beliefs to rational beliefs, you need to think, feel and act in ways that are inconsistent with the former and consistent with the latter.

▶ To get the most out of REBT, you first need to address your disturbed responses to life's adversities or dissatisfactions before dealing effectively with them. Then you are in the best frame of mind to work on developing yourself.

2

Understanding the 'Situational ABC' framework

In this chapter you will learn:
- *the components of REBT's 'Situational ABC' model*
- *what inferences are at 'A'*
- *the key differences between irrational beliefs and rational beliefs*
- *the differential impact of irrational and rational beliefs on the way we feel, behave and think in the face of life's adversities.*

Every approach to counselling and psychotherapy is based on a framework which explains emotional problems and suggests solutions to these problems. REBT is based on a 'Situational ABC' framework which I will discuss in this chapter. I will illustrate my points with the case of Joan who has one of the most common forms of anxiety: public speaking anxiety.

The 'situation'

When you have an emotional problem, you actually experience this problem in specific situations. As we will see, in REBT we recommend analysing these situations one at a time. So, when you take an example of your emotional problem, you will need to begin by describing the situation in which the problem occurred. When you describe the situation, remember the 'four Ws' – where, when, who and what:

Where you were
When you were there
Who else was present
What happened

Joan chose a specific example of her public speaking anxiety to discuss:

Where: I was in a tutorial at College in the tutor's room
When: At 2 p.m. on a Tuesday afternoon
Who: Five students (including me) and the tutor
What: I got anxious and did not say anything.

'A' – the adversity

In REBT, 'A' stands for the aspect of the situation to which the person responds with an unhealthy negative emotion and unconstructive behaviour, for example. In this book, I will call this the 'adversity'. I will discuss how to assess 'A' in Chapter 5.

The most important thing to understand about 'A' is that it is an inference (also known as an interpretation) about what is going on. An inference is a hunch about reality which may be true or false, but goes beyond the data at hand. Let's consider Joan's inference at 'A'.

When Joan came to reflect on the situation outlined above in which she felt anxious, she concluded that she was most anxious about saying something stupid if she chose to speak. This was her adversity. As you can see from what I said above about inferences, the statement 'If I speak, I will say something stupid' is not a fact; rather, it is an inference in that Joan is making a prediction about her future behaviour. She may be correct in her prediction or she may be wrong, and it is this lack of proof one way or the other that makes her statement an inference.

'B' – beliefs

Epictetus, the Roman slave philosopher, is credited with the following saying: 'People are disturbed not by things, but by their views of things.' This is the essence of Cognitive Behaviour Therapy. In REBT, which you will recall is a specific approach within the CBT tradition, these 'views' are known as beliefs. The REBT version of the Epictetus saying is this: 'People are not disturbed by things; rather, they disturb themselves when they hold irrational beliefs about things. When they hold rational beliefs, they respond healthily to things.'

As shown above, REBT theory distinguishes between two types of beliefs: irrational beliefs and rational beliefs. Furthermore, this theory argues that irrational beliefs explain why people have emotional problems about adversities and rational beliefs explain why they have healthy responses to the same adversities.

I will describe irrational beliefs first.

IRRATIONAL BELIEFS

Irrational beliefs are so-called because they have a number of characteristics as first discussed in Chapter 1. They are rigid or extreme, not reality-based, not sensible or logical, and they tend to lead to unhealthy consequences.

In REBT, there are two types of irrational beliefs: rigid beliefs and extreme beliefs. Rigid beliefs are regarded as primary and extreme beliefs (of which there are three) are seen as secondary conclusions from these primary beliefs.

Rigid beliefs
When you hold a rigid belief you not only outline what you want to happen (or don't want to happen), you demand that it *must* happen (or that it *must not* happen). Rigid beliefs take the form of 'musts', 'absolute shoulds', 'have-tos', 'got-tos', etc.

Extreme beliefs
As the name implies, when you hold an extreme belief, you are being extreme in your judgement of yourself, other people or life conditions. In REBT there are three extreme beliefs.

AWFULIZING BELIEFS
When you hold an awfulizing belief you are being extreme in your judgement of an adversity. You are not just saying that it is bad that the adversity has occurred, you are saying that it is awful that it happened. Awfulizing beliefs take the form of 'it's awful that...', 'it's terrible that...' and 'it's the end of the world that...'.

DISCOMFORT INTOLERANCE BELIEFS

When an adversity happens at 'A', and you hold a discomfort intolerance belief, you are extreme in your judgement of your ability to tolerate the adversity. You not only indicate that it is difficult to tolerate the adversity, you hold that you can't tolerate it. Discomfort intolerance beliefs take the form of 'I can't bear it...', 'I can't stand it...' and 'it's intolerable...'.

DEPRECIATION BELIEFS

You can hold a depreciation belief about yourself, about another person or about life conditions. When you do so, you are extreme in your judgement to the extent that you apply a global negative judgement to yourself (e.g. 'I'm worthless'), to the other person (e.g. 'You are a bad person') or to life conditions (e.g. 'Life is bad').

> **Insight**
>
> In REBT, rigid beliefs are primary in determining disturbed responses to adversities. Extreme beliefs (i.e. awfulizing beliefs, discomfort intolerance beliefs and depreciation beliefs) are derived from these rigid beliefs.

CASE STUDY

The case of Joan

Joan held a rigid belief about saying something stupid and an extreme self-depreciation belief that was derived from her rigid belief. Here are her irrational beliefs:

Rigid belief:	*'I must not say something stupid...'*
	↓
Extreme self-depreciation belief:	*'...If I do say something stupid, I am an idiot.'*

RATIONAL BELIEFS

Rational beliefs are so-called because they have a number of characteristics that I first discussed in Chapter 1. They are flexible or non-extreme, reality-based, sensible or logical and they tend to lead to healthy consequences.

In REBT, there are two types of rational beliefs: flexible beliefs and non-extreme beliefs. Flexible beliefs are regarded as primary and non-extreme beliefs (of which there are three) are seen as secondary conclusions from these primary beliefs.

Flexible beliefs

When you hold a flexible belief you outline what you want to happen (or don't want to happen), but you do not demand that it *must* happen (or that it *must not* happen). Flexible beliefs take the form of 'preferences', 'preferential shoulds', 'desires', 'wishes', 'wants', etc. However, a defining characteristic of such flexible beliefs is a full acknowledgement that you do not have to get what you prefer etc.

Non-extreme beliefs

As the name implies, when you hold a non-extreme belief, you are being non-extreme or relative in your judgement of yourself, other people or life conditions. In REBT there are three non-extreme beliefs.

NON-AWFULIZING BELIEFS

When you hold a non-awfulizing belief you are being relative in your judgement of an adversity. You are saying that it is bad, but not awful, that the adversity has occurred. Non-awfulizing beliefs take the form of 'it's bad that...', 'it's unfortunate that...' and 'it's troublesome that...'. However, a defining characteristic of such non-awfulizing beliefs is a full acknowledgement that it is not terrible, awful or the end of the world if the adversity occurs.

DISCOMFORT TOLERANCE BELIEFS

When you encounter an adversity at 'A' and you hold a discomfort tolerance belief about it you are being relative or non-extreme in your judgement of your ability to tolerate the adversity. You accept that, while it is difficult to tolerate the adversity, you can tolerate it and it is worth it to you to do so.

Discomfort tolerance beliefs take the form of 'I can put up with it...', 'I can stand it...' and 'it's tolerable...'. However, a defining characteristic of such discomfort tolerance beliefs is a full acknowledgement that it is worth it to you to bear the adversity, not just that you can do so.

UNCONDITIONAL ACCEPTANCE BELIEFS

You can hold an unconditional acceptance belief about yourself, about another person or about life conditions. When you do so you are again being non-extreme in your judgement to the extent that this acknowledges the complexity, fallibility and fluidity of a person and the complexity and fluidity of life conditions. This judgement is unconditional in nature which means that it remains the same no matter what you do, what the other person does or what happens in life.

It is important to point out that when you hold an unconditional acceptance belief this does not preclude you from making a judgement of an aspect of yourself, of the other person or of life conditions. However, it does mean that you refrain from judging the whole of you, the whole of the other person or the whole of life on the basis of that specific and focused evaluation.

If we look at an unconditional self-acceptance belief, for example, this takes the form of 'I am fallible...', 'I am a unique person...', 'I am acceptable because I am alive...'. However, the defining characteristic of such beliefs is a full acknowledgement that such views are unconditional.

Similar points can be made with reference to an unconditional other-acceptance belief and to an unconditional life-acceptance belief.

> **Insight**
>
> In REBT, flexible beliefs are primary in determining healthy responses to adversities. Non-extreme beliefs (i.e. non-awfulizing beliefs, discomfort tolerance beliefs and acceptance beliefs) are derived from these flexible beliefs.

The case of Joan

Once Joan changed her irrational beliefs to rational beliefs, she held a flexible belief about saying something stupid and a non-extreme unconditional self-acceptance belief that was derived from her flexible belief. Here are her new rational beliefs:

Flexible belief:	*'I would prefer not to say something stupid, but that does not mean that I must not do so.'*
	↓
Non-extreme unconditional self-acceptance belief:	*'I am not an idiot if I do, but an ordinary fallible human being capable of saying sensible and stupid things.'*

'C' – consequences of beliefs about 'A'

In REBT there are three major consequences of beliefs: emotional, behavioural and thinking consequences. In this section, I will begin by considering the consequences of holding irrational beliefs and then I will consider the consequences of holding rational beliefs.

CONSEQUENCES OF HOLDING IRRATIONAL BELIEFS

When people hold rigid and extreme beliefs about adversities at 'A', they will experience three main problematic and unconstructive consequences. I will deal with these one at a time.

Emotional consequences

When people come for counselling it is usually because they are in some kind of emotional pain. As I first explained in Chapter 1, REBT argues that it is important to distinguish between unhealthy negative emotions (UNEs) and healthy negative emotions (HNEs). As the term makes clear, unhealthy negative emotions are those emotions that are negative in tone and unhealthy in effects. When you encounter an adversity, it is important to remember that this is a negative event. It is therefore to be expected that your emotional response will be negative in tone. It is not healthy for you to feel nothing about a negative event, nor is it healthy for you to have a positive emotion about a negative event. So what makes an emotion unhealthy is not that it is negative in tone, but that it is unhealthy in its consequences.

In Chapter 1, I presented a list of the eight major unhealthy negative emotions for which people seek counselling help. Here is a reminder of these emotions: anxiety, depression, guilt, shame, hurt, unhealthy anger, unhealthy jealousy and unhealthy envy.

Behavioural consequences

When you hold irrational beliefs about an adversity, these beliefs will tend to lead you to behave in a largely unconstructive manner. Behavioural consequences of irrational beliefs may be expressed as overt behaviour or as a tendency to act in a certain way which you may or may not transform into actual behaviour. When your belief is irrational and it leads to unconstructive overt behaviour then you will physically do something (such as hit someone when your anger is problematic). However, when your beliefs are irrational, you may also feel like acting in an unhealthy way, but are able to suppress it.

Thus, in unhealthy anger, you may feel like smashing another person in the face, although you don't do so. This is your action tendency that you don't transform into overt behaviour.

When your behaviour is unconstructive (either overt or intended, but not acted on), you tend to:

1 make unhealthy attempts to get rid of accompanying feelings
2 make impulsive attempts to change the adversity
3 make premature attempts to withdraw from the adversity
4 avoid the adversity when facing up to it would be indicated
5 experience a negative impact on your relationships with relevant people
6 experience interruptions to achieving your goals.

Thinking consequences
When you hold irrational beliefs about an adversity these beliefs will tend to lead you subsequently to think in highly distorted and negative ways.

These thoughts are usually inferences (or interpretations), but they differ from the inferences that you make at 'A' in that 'C' inferences are usually more distorted than 'A' inferences. This is because 'C' inferences are the outcome of irrational beliefs and 'A' inferences have not yet been processed by these beliefs.

Insight
Holding irrational beliefs about adversities leads to unhealthy negative emotions, unconstructive behaviour and highly distorted thinking that is heavily skewed to the negative.

The case of Joan

When Joan held irrational beliefs (at 'B') about saying something stupid (at 'A'), her consequences of these irrational beliefs (at 'C') were as follows:

'C' (emotional)   = *Anxiety*

'C' (behavioural)   = *Avoiding saying anything at the tutorial*

'C' (thinking)   = *'If I say something stupid, people will make fun of me for ever.'*

                          = *'My tutor will think I am a hopeless student and will fail me.'*

CONSEQUENCES OF HOLDING RATIONAL BELIEFS

When people hold flexible and non-extreme beliefs about adversities at 'A', they will experience three main healthy and constructive consequences. I will deal with these one at a time.

Emotional consequences

When people face adversities and hold rational beliefs about these adversities, they experience healthy negative emotions. As the term makes clear, healthy negative emotions are those emotions that are negative in tone and healthy in effects.

In Chapter 1, I presented a list of the eight major healthy negative emotions that are the alternatives to the eight major unhealthy negative emotions presented above that people seek counselling help for. Here is a reminder of these healthy negative emotions: concern (rather than anxiety), sadness (rather than depression), remorse (rather than guilt), disappointment (rather than shame), sorrow (rather than hurt), healthy anger (rather than unhealthy anger), healthy jealousy (rather than unhealthy jealousy) and healthy envy (rather than unhealthy envy).

As I noted in Chapter 1, as we have no agreed terms for healthy negative emotions, the terms used above are my own. Feel free to use your own terms if they are more meaningful to you.

Behavioural consequences

When you hold rational beliefs about an adversity these beliefs will tend to lead you to behave (overt actions and action tendencies) in a constructive manner.

When your behaviour is constructive (either overt or intended, but not acted on), you tend to:

1 make healthy attempts to deal with accompanying feelings
2 make considered attempts to change the adversity
3 remain in the presence of the adversity to deal with it rather than withdraw from it
4 face up to the adversity rather than avoid it
5 experience a positive impact on your relationships with relevant people
6 move closer to achieving your goals.

Thinking consequences

When you hold rational beliefs about an adversity these beliefs will tend to lead you subsequently to think in realistic and balanced ways.

> **Insight**
> Holding rational beliefs about adversities leads to healthy negative emotions, constructive behaviour and realistic and balanced thinking.

CASE STUDY

The case of Joan

If Joan were to hold rational beliefs (at 'B') about saying something stupid (at 'A'), her consequences of these rational beliefs (at 'C') will be as follows:

'C' (emotional) = *Concern*

'C' (behavioural) = *Speaking up in the tutorial*

'C' (thinking) = *'If I say something stupid, perhaps one person might make fun of me for ever, but most won't.'*

= *'My tutor will think I have taken a risk and that I have much to learn, but he probably won't think that I am a hopeless student and I doubt very much that he will fail me.'*

In the next chapter I will provide an overview of how to tackle one of your problems using REBT.

THINGS TO REMEMBER

▶ You experience your emotional problems in specific situations.

▶ What you are most disturbed about in a specific situation is often a key inference that you make about what happened (or what did not happen) in that situation.

▶ Irrational beliefs comprise rigid beliefs and extreme beliefs.

▶ Rational beliefs comprise flexible beliefs and non-extreme beliefs.

▶ Rigid beliefs are at the core of our disturbed responses (emotional, behavioural and thinking) to adversities and we derive our extreme belief conclusions from these rigid beliefs.

▶ Flexible beliefs are at the core of our healthy responses (emotional, behavioural and thinking) to adversities and we derive our non-extreme belief conclusions from these flexible beliefs.

3

....

Tackling your problems: an overview

In this chapter you will learn:
- *the general steps you need to take while tackling your emotional problems using REBT*
- *the general principles of assessing your problems*
- *the importance of questioning both your irrational and rational beliefs and strengthening your rational beliefs*
- *that obstacles to change are an expected part of the change process and that you need to be ready to deal with these obstacles.*

In this chapter I provide an overview of the steps that you will take when you use this book to tackle one of your emotional problems. You may have more than one problem, of course, and I will deal with this issue in Chapter 11. However, the best way of judging how you can use REBT in practice is to see how you can apply it with one problem at a time. While I will outline a number of steps that I think you will need to take, and will do so in a particular order, I want to make clear at the outset that you should use only the steps that make sense to you and in the order in which you deem most helpful. I am certainly not suggesting that you use the following steps slavishly in the order that I discuss them.

Wherever relevant, I will illustrate my points with reference to the case of Joan whom we first met in Chapter 2.

Step 1: Admit that you have an emotional problem

Unless you admit to yourself that you have an emotional problem, then you will obviously not do anything to help yourself, since you do not think that you need help. If you have an emotional problem, you will experience debilitating emotional pain accompanied by a sense of being stuck in a way of thinking, feeling and behaving which has an unhealthy effect on your life and interferes with you working towards your goals. If you have an emotional problem, then the main reason why you will not admit this to yourself is that you feel ashamed of having the problem. Shame, in this context, stems from the irrational belief that 'I must be strong and in control and I am a defective person if I am not'.

For you to admit that you have an emotional problem, therefore, you need to see that you are not a defective person for having the problem. Rather, you are an ordinary person who is not immune from having emotional problems. Developing this attitude will lead you to admit to having an emotional problem and to take the next step.

The case of Joan

Joan readily admitted to herself that she had a problem with speaking in public and decided to seek help for this problem.

Step 2: Assess a specific example of your emotional problem

In order to tackle your emotional problem, you need to understand it. Taking a specific example of this problem is the best initial step you can take to do this. Then you need to use the 'Situational ABC' framework – discussed in Chapter 2 – to provide you with the necessary information to help you to address the problem.

Thus, you need to take the specific example and do the following:

▶ Describe the 'situation' in which your problem occurred.
▶ Identify 'C'. This will be the major problematic emotion you experienced in this situation along with what you did (or felt like doing) and your associated thinking.

▶ Identify your 'A'. Remember that 'A' stands for 'adversity' and will be the aspect of the situation about which you were most disturbed.

▶ Identify your irrational beliefs at 'B'. These will be a rigid belief and at least one extreme belief that, taken together, account for your responses at 'C' to 'A'. This step is particularly important because it helps you to understand that your emotional problem is not caused by the adversity. Rather, your emotional problem stems from the irrational beliefs that you hold *about* the adversity.

The case of Joan

As I showed in Chapter 2, Joan chose a recent, specific example of her problem which we assessed as follows:

Joan's problem-based 'Situational ABC'		
'Situation'	=	*I was in a tutorial at College in the tutor's room at 2 p.m. on a Tuesday afternoon. Five students (including me) and the tutor were present*
'A'	=	*'If I speak in the tutorial, I will say something stupid.'*
'B' (irrational)	=	*'I must not say something stupid in the tutorial and I am an idiot if I do.'*
'C' (emotional)	=	*Anxiety*
'C' (behavioural)	=	*Avoiding saying anything at the tutorial*
'C' (thinking)	=	*'If I say something stupid, people in the tutorial will make fun of me for ever.'*
	=	*'My tutor will think I am a hopeless student and will fail me.'*

Insight

If you understand the factors that explain your emotional problem, you will be able to address it effectively. The 'Situational ABC' framework enables you to do this.

Step 3: Set goals

Once you have assessed the specific example of your problem, it is important that you have a clear idea of what constitutes a healthy way of responding to the same adversity at 'A'. Here, it is important that you choose a goal that is realistic and to which you can commit yourself. Ideally this goal should comprise healthy emotional, behavioural and thinking responses.

It is also important for you to see that these healthy responses are underpinned by alternative rational beliefs at 'B'. These beliefs will comprise a flexible belief (the healthy alternative to your rigid belief) and your main non-extreme belief (a healthy alternative to your main extreme belief).

The case of Joan

In what follows, I will present Joan's new 'Situational ABC' which shows her goals. I call this her goal-based 'Situational ABC'. Please note the following:

▶ Joan's 'Situation' and 'A' in her goal-based 'Situational ABC' are the same as in her problem-based 'Situational ABC'.
▶ Joan's rational belief has yet to be assessed.
▶ Joan's 'C' in her goal-based 'Situational ABC' is different to her 'C' in the problem-based 'Situational ABC'.

Joan's goal-based 'Situational ABC'

'Situation'	=	*I was in a tutorial at College in the tutor's room at 2 p.m. on a Tuesday afternoon. Five students (including me) and the tutor were present*
'A'	=	*'If I speak in the tutorial, I will say something stupid.'*
'B' (rational)	=	*To be identified*
'C' (emotional)	=	*Concern*
'C' (behavioural)	=	*Speaking at the tutorial*

(Contd)

| 'C' (thinking) | = | 'If I say something stupid, perhaps one person might make fun of me, but most won't.' |
| | = | 'My tutor will think I have taken a risk and that I have much to learn, but he probably won't think that I am a hopeless student and I doubt very much that he will fail me.' |

Step 4: Identify your rational beliefs and see that these will help you to achieve your goals

Once you have set goals, you need to see that the best way to achieve these goals is to develop alternatives to the irrational beliefs that underpin your problems. This involves you:

▶ developing a flexible belief as an alternative to your rigid belief
▶ developing a non-extreme belief as an alternative to the extreme belief that, together with your rigid belief, was most responsible for your disturbance. If this was an awfulizing belief, develop a non-awfulizing belief; if it was a discomfort intolerance belief, develop a discomfort tolerance belief; and if it was a depreciation belief, develop the appropriate acceptance belief (see Chapter 2).

Once you have developed rational alternatives to your irrational beliefs, it is important that you understand that these will help you to achieve the goals that you specified in Step 3 above.

The case of Joan

Joan developed the following rational belief alternatives to her irrational beliefs:

Rigid belief	Alternative flexible belief
'I must not say something stupid in the tutorial.'	'I would prefer not to say something stupid, but that does not mean that I must not do so.'

Self-depreciation belief	Alternative unconditional self-acceptance belief
'If I say something stupid in the tutorial I am an idiot.'	*'If I say something stupid in the tutorial, I am not an idiot. I am a fallible human being capable of saying intelligent, stupid and neutral things.'*

Joan understood how these beliefs, if she believed them, would help her achieve the goals that she set in Step 3.

Insight

If you know what constitutes a healthy alternative to your problem and how to reach this alternative, then you will increase the chances of dealing effectively with this problem than if you lack this knowledge.

Step 5: Question your beliefs

Here, you need to question your irrational beliefs and your rational beliefs. The purpose of this questioning process is twofold:

1 First, it helps you to understand that your irrational beliefs are false, illogical and unhelpful in general and, more specifically, prevent you from achieving your goal of responding healthily to the adversity.
2 Second, it helps you to understand that your rational beliefs are true, logical and helpful in general and, more specifically, increase your chances of achieving your goal of responding healthily to the adversity.

The case of Joan

Through questioning her irrational and rational beliefs, Joan came to see that her rigid and self-depreciation beliefs were false and illogical and had resulted only in her maintaining her problem rather than in solving it. She also saw that her flexible and unconditional self-acceptance beliefs were true and logical and would help her to solve her problem.

Step 6: Strengthen your conviction in your rational beliefs and weaken your conviction in your irrational beliefs

Just understanding that your irrational beliefs are irrational (i.e. false, illogical and unhelpful) and that your rational beliefs are rational (true, logical and helpful) is usually not sufficient to change your irrational beliefs. In order to change these beliefs, it is important that you act and think in ways that are consistent with your developing rational beliefs and inconsistent with your currently held irrational beliefs.

You will need to commit yourself to this process of changing your beliefs until your feelings change to catch up with your healthy behaviour and thinking. To paraphrase Gandhi, you deal healthily with an adversity when there is consistency among your beliefs, behaviour, emotions and subsequent thinking with respect to the adversity.

The case of Joan

Joan understood that she had to 'walk the talk' and not just 'talk the talk' when it came to her rational beliefs. This meant, in her case, speaking up at every opportunity in tutorials while rehearsing her rational beliefs and doing so until she felt duly concerned, but not anxious, about the prospect of saying something stupid in class.

Step 7: Generalize your learning

So far, I have discussed what you need to do in order to deal with a typical and specific example of your emotional problem. In order to generalize your learning you need to do two things:

1 Deal with other examples of your emotional problem when you encounter them using the same process of change that you employed in dealing with your selected typical and specific example.
2 Look for a general theme that appears in examples of your emotional problem. You will normally be able to find this when you look at 'A' in your 'Situational ABCs'. In Table 3.1 below I list common themes that are associated with the eight major emotional problems for which people seek help.

Table 3.1 Common themes associated with unhealthy negative emotions.

Theme of the adversity at 'A'	Emotional problem at 'C'
Threat	Anxiety
Loss / failure	Depression
Breaking your moral code; failing to live up to your moral code; hurting someone	Guilt
Falling very short of your ideal in a social context	Shame
Someone betrays you or lets you down and you think you do not deserve such treatment	Hurt
Self or other transgresses a personal rule; other threatens self-esteem; frustration	Unhealthy anger
Threat to valued relationship	Unhealthy jealousy
Others have what you value and lack	Unhealthy envy

Once you have found the theme, add your rigid demand and the major extreme belief that accounts for your problem and this becomes your core irrational belief. Then you need to develop an alternative core rational belief that comprises the theme plus a flexible belief and most appropriate non-extreme belief. Once you have done this you can use this core rational belief as a guide to think rationally as you face up to the adversities defined by the theme and act in ways that are consistent with this belief. I will deal with this topic in greater detail in Chapter 11.

The case of Joan

Joan dealt with a number of examples where she was anxious about speaking up in public. She dealt with these by using the 'Situational ABC' framework to assess the episodes, by questioning her beliefs

(Contd)

to establish her rational beliefs and by acting on them to strengthen them. She identified the following core irrational belief and its healthy alternative from this work:

Joan's core irrational belief	Joan's alternative core rational belief
'I must come across intelligently to people who matter and if I don't then I am worthless.'	*'I want to come across intelligently to those who matter, but I really don't have to do so. If I don't, then I am not worthless. I am a fallible complex person whose worth is determined by my humanity not by how intelligently I come across to people.'*

Joan used her core rational belief to talk to people who matter to her when there was a risk that she may not come across intelligently. As she did this over time, she became more relaxed in social situations.

Step 8: Deal with obstacles to change

When you resolve to act in ways that are consistent with your developing rational beliefs, you may not always do so. It is important that you identify and deal with these obstacles to change if you are going to deal effectively with your emotional problem. I will deal with this issue in greater detail in Chapter 14.

The case of Joan

When Joan first resolved to speak up in a tutorial while rehearsing her rational beliefs she did not do so. This was because she did not feel confident about what she wanted to say. It transpired that she held a rigid belief about confidence that proved to be an obstacle to change. She dealt with this by showing herself that, while it would be good if she felt confident before speaking up, she did not have to have such confidence and that repeatedly speaking in tutorials while being unconfident is the best way of developing such confidence.

Step 9: Dealing with lapses and relapse

Psychological change, like the course of true love, rarely runs smoothly. Having made progress we may take steps backwards and, if we do not deal with these lapses, we will relapse and go back to square one. If you accept that, at times, you will take steps back this will help you to learn from such lapses and as a result you will minimize the chances that you will relapse.

Another good way of minimizing the chances of relapse is to identify and deal with vulnerability factors. These are so called because they are factors that, if not dealt with, will mean that you are vulnerable to experiencing your problem. Such factors may be located in your environment (e.g. seeing other people smoking when you are trying to give up), to do with other people (e.g. people being rude to you when you are dealing with your need for approval) or to do with yourself (e.g. being bored when you are dealing with your tendency to overeat). If you can face up to these factors in a stepwise manner while rehearsing appropriate rational beliefs, then you will be successful at dealing with your vulnerability factors. I will deal with such issues in greater detail in Chapter 12.

The case of Joan

Once Joan realized that she could speak unconfidently in tutorials she spoke up regularly. However, she realized that on the occasion that she did not do so, it was when the tutor was known to be particularly critical. Having identified this as a vulnerability factor, Joan refined her rational belief to deal with this adversity and acted on this refined rational belief with all but the most critical tutor at college of whom virtually all the students were scared.

CASE STUDY

....

Insight
Expect to encounter obstacles along the way to personal change and develop a plan to overcome them.
....

Step 10: Deal with any distortions of 'A'

When you are dealing with a specific example of your problem, but normally after you have identified, challenged and changed your irrational beliefs, you need to revisit your adversity at 'A' to determine whether or not it was realistic or distorted. If your 'A' is distorted and you correct this distortion before you have identified and dealt with your irrational beliefs, you will only help yourself in the short-term since, according to REBT, your emotional problem is determined largely by these beliefs and not by any distortions that you may have made at 'A'. I will deal with this topic in greater detail in Chapter 10.

The case of Joan

After she had identified and challenged her irrational beliefs, but before she had acted on her developing rational beliefs, Joan revisited her 'A' and realized that it was by no means certain that she would say something stupid if she spoke in a tutorial. However, she also realized that it was possible for her to do so and therefore she still needed to think rationally about this prospect even though it was now a possibility rather than a certainty.

In this and the previous chapter I have laid the foundations for how you can modify your thinking and change your behaviour when they serve to largely determine and maintain your emotional problem. In Chapters 3–10, I will build on these foundations to consider the nuts and bolts of doing so.

THINGS TO REMEMBER

▶ When tackling your emotional problems it's best to do so one at a time.

▶ When tackling a specific emotional problem, it's best to start with a specific example of this problem using the 'Situational ABC' framework.

▶ It's important to set goals so that you know what you are aiming for in tackling your problems.

▶ It's important that you understand that your irrational beliefs underpin your problem and their rational belief alternatives will help you to achieve your goals.

▶ Questioning your beliefs will help you to understand that your irrational beliefs are irrational and their rational alternatives are rational.

▶ Acting and thinking in ways that are consistent with your rational beliefs will help to strengthen your conviction in them.

▶ The path to dealing effectively with your emotional problems is rarely smooth and you should expect lapses and obstacles along the way.

▶ You are advised to develop plans to respond constructively when you lapse and encounter obstacles to change.

▶ You are best advised to question the validity of your inferences at 'A' when you have dealt with your emotional disturbance at 'C'.

4

....

Identifying and formulating your problems and goals

In this chapter you will learn:
- *why identifying your problems and goals is so important*
- *two approaches to identifying and formulating your problems and goals and their similarities and differences.*

In discussing the issues related to identifying problems and goals, I will use the case example of Harvey who had several problems that he wanted to address using the material presented in this book.

The importance of identifying your problems and goals

Dr Aaron T. Beck, the founder of Cognitive Therapy, an approach that is quite similar to Rational Emotive Behaviour Therapy, stressed that in the early phase of Cognitive Therapy it is very useful for the therapist to help the client to make a problem list. Such a list includes all the problems that the client has and wants to address in the course of therapy. This list is not set in stone and can be modified in the course of therapy. I suggest that you can get the most out of this book if you too develop a problem list; I will discuss two approaches to this issue in due course.

Now as you develop a problem list it is also useful for you to consider what you would like to achieve in addressing these problems. These are, in effect, your *goals*. Most practitioners in the Cognitive Behaviour Therapy (CBT) tradition would agree that it is good to have something to work towards in therapy and self-help. It provides a direction for the process and helps prevent you from floundering around, not knowing where you are headed.

Putting your problems and goals into your own words

Putting your problems and goals into your own words is important in that you are starting within your frame of reference. Later on in this chapter I will suggest a formula that you can use based on REBT that will help you get the most from this book. However, if I started with such an approach without giving you an opportunity to express yourself in your own way with respect to your problems and goals, you would get the impression that I wasn't interested in how you see things from your own perspective and this is certainly not the case. So let's start with you putting your problems into your own words.

PUTTING YOUR PROBLEMS INTO YOUR OWN WORDS

When you put your problems into your own words, it is important to be as concise as possible. Long rambling descriptions of your concerns may be cathartic, but they will probably contain too much information when what is needed is a concise summary of each of your problems. Try to only use a sentence and a short one at that.

The case of Harvey

Here is the list of problems that Harvey developed using his own words. Note the short summary nature of each problem. This is what you should aim for when developing your own problem list.

Harvey's problems in his own words:

1 *Anxious about working on my dissertation*
2 *Guilty about not visiting my parents often enough*
3 *Want to break up with my girlfriend but scared of hurting her feelings*
4 *Procrastinate on doing household chores*
5 *Anxious at social gatherings so tend not to talk.*

PUTTING YOUR GOALS INTO YOUR OWN WORDS

As with your problems, when you put your goals into your own words, it is equally important to be as concise as possible. Otherwise, by providing too much information about what you would like you may miss the wood because there are too many trees. Again, try to use only a short sentence.

Also, when you specify your goals be as realistic as possible and only state goals that are in your power to achieve. Don't include changes in others as goals as these are not within your control to achieve. You can *influence* others – in which case state these influence attempts as your goal – but you can't *change* them!

The case of Harvey

Here is the list of goals that Harvey developed using his own words. Note the short summary nature of each goal. This is again what you should aim for when developing your own goals list.

Harvey's goals in his own words:

1 To *work on my dissertation without feeling anxious*
2 To *accept that I am very busy and can't visit my parents as often as I would like*
3 *Want to tell my girlfriend that I want to break up with her without hurting her feelings*
4 To *stop procrastinating on doing household chores*
5 To *talk to people at social gatherings without being anxious.*

Insight
When you put your problems and goals in your own words, you build commitment to tackling the former and pursuing the latter.

Formulating your problems and goals using REBT

Now that you have put your problems and goals into your own words, you are ready to formulate them using insights derived from REBT. Doing this will enable you to get the most out of REBT since by formulating your problems and goals you make them more precise and when they are more precise they are easier to work with. In what follows, I will be drawing on the 'Situational ABC' framework that I first described in Chapter 2 and you might find it useful to re-read that chapter before you use the following steps.

FORMULATE YOUR EMOTIONAL PROBLEMS

I suggest that you use the following steps in formulating each of your emotional problems:

['Situations'] – Identify the situations in which you experience your problem.

['A'] – Identify the theme of the problem. Ask yourself what is it about the situations that you specified that is a problem for you. This is likely to be an inference. Consult Table 3.1 for help on this point.

['C' (Emotional)] – Identify the one major unhealthy negative emotion that you experience when you encounter the situations and theme that you specified above.

['C' (Behavioural)] – Identify the dysfunctional behaviour that you demonstrate in these situations.

['C' (Thinking)] – Identify the thinking you engage in once your unhealthy negative emotion has 'kicked in'.

The case of Harvey

Here is how Harvey used the above structure to formulate one of his problems: 'Anxious about working on my dissertation'.

Type of situation: *Any time I plan to start work on my dissertation* ['Situations']

Theme: *I think that the work that I will do won't be very creative* ['A']

Major unhealthy negative emotion: *Anxious* ['C' (Emotional)]

Behaviour: *I put off starting work on the dissertation* ['C' (Behavioural)]

Thinking: *'I will fail my dissertation and will end up on skid row'* ['C' (Thinking)]

Putting this into a sentence we have:

'Any time I plan to start work on my dissertation, I think that the work that I will do on it won't be very creative. I feel anxious
(Contd)

about this, put off starting work on it and think that I will fail my dissertation and will end up on skid row.'

Comparing Harvey's 'own words'- based problem with his formulated problem

The following contrasts Harvey's 'own words'-based problem with his REBT-inspired formulated problem.

Harvey's 'own words' approach	Harvey's 'formulated' approach
Anxious about working on my dissertation	'Any time I plan to start work on my dissertation, I think that the work that I will do won't be very creative. I feel anxious and put off starting work on the dissertation. I also think that I will fail my dissertation and will end up on skid row.'

If you look carefully at this table, you will note the following:

▶ Both approaches mention that Harvey is anxious.
▶ Both approaches mention that Harvey is anxious about his dissertation, but the formulated approach specifies more what he is most anxious about – not being very creative.

Only the formulated approach outlines the behavioural and thinking aspects of the problem at 'C'.

FORMULATE YOUR GOALS

I suggest that you use the following steps in formulating each of your goals:

[**Situations**] – Identify the situations in which you experience your problem. This will be the same as you listed in the 'situations' section of your formulated problem above.
[**'A'**] – Identify the theme of the problem. Ask yourself what is it about the situations that you specified that is a problem for you. This is likely to be an inference and will be the same as you listed under 'A' in your formulated problem above.

['C' (**Emotional Goal**)] – Identify the healthy alternative to the major unhealthy negative emotion that you experienced when you encountered the situations and theme that you specified above. Note that this emotional goal should be negative because it is about an adversity, but it should also be healthy in the sense that it will enable you to deal effectively with the adversity if it can be changed or to adjust constructively to it if it cannot be changed.

['C' (**Behavioural Goal**)] – Identify the functional alternative to the unconstructive behaviour that you demonstrated.

['C' (**Thinking Goal**)] – Identify the realistic alternative to the highly distorted thinking that you engaged in.

The case of Harvey

Here is how Harvey used the above structure to formulate one of his goals: 'To work on my dissertation without feeling anxious'.

Type of situation: *Any time I plan to start work on my dissertation* ['Situations']

Theme: *I think that the work that I will do won't be very creative* ['A']

Major healthy negative emotion: *To feel concern (rather than anxious)*
['C' (Emotional Goal)]

Behaviour: *To get down to work on my dissertation (rather than procrastinate)*
['C' (Behavioural Goal)]

Thinking: *'To think that my dissertation may fail, but equally that it may not. Also to recognize that my thought that I may end up on skid row is just a thought and is unlikely to happen' (rather than to see failing and ending up on skid row as being inevitable)*
['C' (Thinking Goal)]

Putting this into a sentence we have:

'Any time I plan to start work on my dissertation, I think that the work that I will do won't be very creative. I want to feel

(Contd)

concern (rather than anxious) about it and to get down to work on the dissertation (rather than procrastinate). I want to think that my dissertation may fail, but equally that it may not. Also to recognize that my thought that I may end up on skid row is just a thought and is unlikely to happen (rather than to think that failure and ending up on skid row is inevitable).'

> **Insight**
> When you use REBT theory to formulate your problems and goals, you get the most out of what this approach to therapy has to offer in laying the foundations for dealing effectively with these problems.

Comparing Harvey's 'own words'-based goal with his formulated goal

The following table contrasts Harvey's 'own words'- based goal with his REBT-inspired formulated goal.

Harvey's 'own words' goal	Harvey's 'formulated' goal
To work on my dissertation without feeling anxious	*'Any time I plan to start work on my dissertation, I think that the work that I will do won't be very creative. I want to feel concern (rather than anxious) about it and to get down to work on the dissertation (rather than putting off starting work on it). I want to think that my dissertation may fail, but equally that it may not. Also I want to recognize that my thought that I may end up on skid row is just that, a thought, and is unlikely to happen.'*

If you look carefully at this table, you will note the following:

▶ In the 'own words' approach, Harvey expresses his behavioural goal (i.e. to work on his dissertation) and that he does not want to experience anxiety; whereas in the formulated approach, Harvey specifies his emotional, behavioural and thinking goals.

▶ In the 'own words' approach, Harvey does not mention his 'A', but does so in the formulated approach (i.e. not being very creative in his dissertation).

Note that when you formulate goals for your emotional problems, you are changing only your emotional, behavioural and thinking responses to the situations and theme in these situations that you find problematic. This is because in REBT we want you to be prepared to face life's adversities even when you think that an adversity will happen when in fact it doesn't.

Also, note that under the headings of 'emotional goal', 'behavioural goal' and 'thinking goal', I suggest that you use the 'rather than' wording to highlight the difference between your problem response and your goal response. However, if you find doing this cumbersome, then omit the 'rather than' phrases.

In the next chapter I will discuss choosing and working with a target problem and a specific example of that problem.

THINGS TO REMEMBER

▶ When identifying your problems and goals develop such a list, putting them into your own words.

▶ After you have done this, use REBT theory to formulate these problems and goals.

▶ When formulating a problem select your main unhealthy negative emotion at 'C'. Also identify the behavioural 'Cs' and thinking 'Cs' that go along with this emotional 'C'.

▶ When formulating a problem, identify the situations in which you experience the problem and the major theme at 'A'. The 'A' is what you are most disturbed about.

▶ When formulating a goal, remember that the situations and the theme at 'A' are the same as in your formulated problem. Only your emotion, behaviour and thinking at 'C' are different.

5

Selecting and working with a target problem and a specific example of that problem

In this chapter you will learn:
- *the importance of working on one problem at a time*
- *how to select a problem to work on – known as a target problem*
- *the importance of keeping your focus on the target problem as you use the process of REBT*
- *the importance of selecting a specific example of your target problem to work with.*

In the previous chapter I suggested that you develop a problem and goal list. This list contains all the emotional problems that you have that you want to address and your initial idea of what you want to achieve by addressing them. I then helped you to formulate each problem and related goal using REBT theory. Having done this, you are ready to tackle your problems one at a time. Throughout this chapter I will make reference to the case of Harvey whom we first met in Chapter 4.

Selecting a target problem

You may be thinking, why work on my problems one at a time? Why not work on them all at once or in batches? There are a number of reasons why I suggest that you work on one problem especially at the beginning of the self-change process:

▶ **Don't be a tired clown!** Have you ever been to the circus and watched a clown try to keep eight saucers spinning on eight long sticks? All is well at the beginning, but after a while the clown becomes tired and eventually all the plates come crashing to earth. If you try to deal with all your problems at once (or even in smaller batches), you will eventually become exhausted and will end up not helping yourself with any of your problems. So, selecting and dealing with one problem at a time, at least initially, helps you not become a tired clown!

▶ **Don't be a confused horse – wear blinkers!** If you try to deal with all your problems at once (or even in smaller batches), you will quite soon become quite confused and your mind will wander from one problem to the next and back again. Some racehorses wear blinkers. Why? Because otherwise their attention will wander and they will not be able to do their best in the race. Wearing blinkers helps them to focus. Likewise, selecting and working with one problem at a time will help you to focus and get the best out of REBT.

▶ **Focusing helps you to learn new skills!** Throughout this book, I am going to teach you and help you learn new skills. If you implement and practise these skills you will increase the chances that you will help yourself address your emotional problems effectively. Learning any new skill is usually difficult and you will maximize the chances of learning the skills in this book if you focus on one problem at a time without the added distraction of dealing with two or more problems at once.

When you have chosen a problem to work on this is known as your **target problem**. The term 'target problem' can best be thought of as the problem you have targeted to work on first.

CRITERIA FOR SELECTING YOUR TARGET PROBLEM

If you are not clear which problem you should select as your target problem, then let me suggest the following criteria that you might find helpful.

Current preoccupation

You may wish to select as your target problem that problem with which you are currently preoccupied. The advantage of this criterion is that you are working on a problem where your focus is naturally. However, this problem may be very difficult to address or may not be suitable to tackle first for other reasons and thus you may not choose to select it as your target problem.

Easiest to tackle

You may wish to select as your target problem that problem for your list that is, in your view, easiest to tackle. On the grounds that nothing succeeds better than success, if you are able to deal with your easiest problem then you may develop the confidence to address a more complex problem. Of course, if you target your easiest problem and do not succeed in addressing it successfully, you may well become discouraged about applying REBT to your problems.

Engenders hope

Finally, you may wish to select as your target problem that problem from your list that if you address effectively will inspire you with hope for the future. Again the danger is that if you do not address it effectively, you may become hopeless.

I suggest that you consider the above criteria and ask yourself which criterion is likely to help you in the long run. Choose the criterion that you resonate with the most and use this to select your target problem.

....

Insight

You will get the most out of REBT if you work on one problem at a time.

....

The case of Harvey

In Chapter 4 I discussed how to formulate one of Harvey's problems and related goals. This problem (as stated in Harvey's own words) was as follows: *Anxious about working on my dissertation.* Harvey chose this problem to be his target problem.

Working with the target problem all the way through

In the television quiz *Mastermind*, when the quizmaster, John Humphrys, has started asking a question, but is interrupted by the end of round buzzer, he responds: 'I've started, so I'll finish.' This is sound advice when it comes to working on your target problem. So, once you have selected a target problem, it is best if you continue with it rather than 'chopping and changing' and going from one problem to the next without achieving closure on the target problem.

Having made this general point, there are, of course, exceptions to this rule. I will mention two:

1 Remain with the target problem, unless another problem has come to occupy your mental space and you cannot sufficiently 'park' this other problem. In which case change to this problem.
2 Remain with the target problem unless another problem has emerged that is far more serious than the target problem. Again, if this happens change to this problem.

However, if you find that you keep changing from problem to problem despite resolving to sticking with one, then you may need some professional assistance to help you understand the reasons for this continual shifting from problem to problem. Once this issue has been resolved and you can work with your target problem over time then you can resume using this book for self-help purposes.

> **Insight**
> Unless there is good reason not to do so, keep working on your target problem until you have dealt effectively with it.

Selecting a specific example of the target problem

Once you have selected a particular problem to work on from your problem list, it is particularly important that you follow on from this by selecting a specific example of this problem to work on. In Chapter 2 I presented the 'Situational ABC' framework which has been designed to help you to understand your problems in their situational context. I pointed out in that chapter that we experience our problems in specific situations and therefore working with a specific example of your target problem will help you to understand the 'ABC' of your problem as you actually experience it – i.e. in a specific situational context.

Thus, a specific example of your target problem is one where you can provide the following information as I discussed in Chapter 2:

Where you were
When you were there
Who else was present
What happened.

Here are some suggestions about selecting a specific example of your target problem.

SELECT AN EMOTIONALLY LADEN EXAMPLE OF YOUR TARGET PROBLEM

It is best if you pick a specific example that is fresh in your mind and one that has emotional resonance for you. If you are likely to feel the disturbed emotion (at 'C') as you focus on the event then so much the better, as experiencing the emotion (at 'C') will enable you to identify the other elements of the 'ABC' model more easily than if you experience no emotion as you focus on the event.

SELECT A TYPICAL EXAMPLE OF YOUR TARGET PROBLEM

A typical example of your target problem is one that occurs frequently. As such you may have many examples to choose from, which is an advantage. However, there is also the danger, if you are not careful, of fusing two or more examples in your mind, with the result that your resultant 'fused' example loses its emotional impact and the information that you are likely to give about 'ABC' factors in your 'fused' example is likely to be theoretical. To guard against this, use the 'where, when, who, what' framework in working with a typical example of your target problem.

SELECT A RECENT EXAMPLE OF YOUR TARGET PROBLEM

The advantage of selecting a recent example of your target problem is that, as it is recent, you should be able to recall it without too much difficulty. However, if the example is not very memorable or if some of the problem's main features may not be present, it is best not to use a recent example.

SELECT A VIVID EXAMPLE OF YOUR TARGET PROBLEM

A vivid example of your target problem is one that stands out in your mind. It will therefore probably provide you with emotionally laden information that will enable you to identify more easily the relevant 'ABC' factors. However, because it is vivid it may not be representative of your problem as you normally experience it. Bear this in mind when thinking about selecting a vivid example of your target problem.

SELECT AN IMMINENT EXAMPLE OF YOUR TARGET PROBLEM

An imminent example of your target problem is one that has not actually occurred yet, but that you predict will occur in the foreseeable future. The main advantage of selecting an imminent example of your target problem is that it gives self-help a forward-looking impetus and helps you to choose a relevant homework assignment (see Chapter 8) so that you face up to your predicted adversity and practise the skills that I will teach you later in the book. Using imminent examples of your target problem is particularly useful for anxiety problems and for dealing with procrastination or other forms of avoidance.

The main disadvantage of selecting an imminent example of your target problem is that, as the event has not yet happened, you may not be able to envision with sufficient clarity the specific event that exists only in your mind.

In summary, the very best specific example of your target problem is one that is:

▶ recent or imminent
▶ emotionally laden
▶ vivid *and*
▶ typical.

The more of these factors you can incorporate in your selected specific example, the better.

The worst specific example you can choose is one that:

▶ has happened long ago or you think will happen far into the future
▶ has little present emotional impact on you
▶ is unclear *and*
▶ is untypical.

The fewer of these factors you can incorporate in your selected specific example, the better.

> **Insight**
> Working with a *specific* example of your target problem brings therapy to life.

The case of Harvey

Harvey chose a typical, imminent example of his target problem. He was planning to work on his dissertation at 5.30 p.m. that evening in his study, but he thought that it was unlikely that he would get down to doing any work on his dissertation.

In the following chapter I will discuss using the 'Situational ABC' framework to assess a chosen example of a target problem and to set goals for this problem.

THINGS TO REMEMBER

▶ Selecting and working on one problem at a time will help you get the most out of REBT.

▶ When selecting a target problem choose one (1) with which you are currently preoccupied; (2) that is easiest to tackle or (3) that will engender the most hope in you.

▶ Once you have selected a target problem, keep your focus on this problem until you have dealt effectively with it. Only change focus if you are preoccupied with another emotional problem and you can't concentrate on the target problem or something far more serious has happened to you which needs urgent attention.

▶ Selecting a specific example of your target problem will help you assess your problem in greater detail.

▶ When you select a specific example, choose one that is emotionally laden, typical, vivid and recent or imminent.

6

Using the 'Situational ABC' framework to assess your specific example and to set goals

In this chapter you will learn:
- *how to use the 'Situational ABC' framework to assess the specific example of your target problem that you have selected and to set an appropriate goal for that example*
- *how to use an instruction-based self-help form designed to be employed with specific examples of target problems.*

While reading the steps that I discuss in this chapter, I suggest that you refer to the self-help form that I present in Appendix 1. You may wish to use this form from now on. However, feel free to modify it or even construct your own form.

Once again, in this chapter I will illustrate my points with reference to Harvey. Harvey's completed form will be presented at the end of the chapter in Table 6.5.

Give a brief description of the 'situation'

As I pointed out in Chapter 2, you experience your emotional problems in specific situations even if these situations are in your mind. Your task here is to write down on the form, under the heading 'Situation', a brief, objective description of the 'situation' you were in when you disturbed yourself. As I discussed in Chapters 2 and 5, it is useful to keep in mind the following 'Ws' when describing the situation:

Where you were
When you were there

Who else was present
What happened.

The case of Harvey

If you recall, Harvey's target problem that he expressed in his own words was that he was anxious about working on his dissertation. He chose the following specific example of this problem: *'I have made plans to work on my dissertation at 5.30 p.m. tonight in my study, but it is unlikely that I will do so.'*

Identify 'C'

After you have described the 'situation', the next step is to focus on the responses that comprised your emotional problem. These are placed at 'C' in the 'Situational ABC' framework. You may be wondering at this point why I am suggesting that you start with 'C' and not with 'A'. In my experience, knowing your disturbed emotion at 'C' helps you to identify 'A' more easily than knowing your 'A' helps you to identify 'C'. However, as the form shows, the steps where you identify 'A' and 'C' are interchangeable, and if you want to identify 'A' before 'C', that's fine.

You will remember from Chapter 2 that there are three types of 'C' that we are interested in: the *emotional*, *behavioural* and *thinking* consequences of your irrational beliefs.

Let me consider these one at a time.

IDENTIFY YOUR MAJOR UNHEALTHY NEGATIVE EMOTION (UNE)

Here are some tips to help you to identify your major UNE.

Look at your formulated problem for your specific unhealthy negative emotion

In Chapter 4 I showed you how to formulate your problems in general terms. So, when you experience one of your formulated problems in a specific situation, it should be easy to identify your specific UNE – it will be substantially the same emotion as the one listed in your formulated problem.

> Your unhealthy negative emotion indicates the theme of what you are
> disturbed about and it also tells you that your belief is irrational.

The case of Harvey

For example, Harvey's formulated problem was:

> *'Any time I plan to start work on my dissertation, I think that
> the work that I will do on it won't be very creative. I feel anxious
> about this, put off starting work on it and think that I will fail
> my dissertation and will end up on skid row.'*

The 'situation' in Harvey's specific example was as follows:

> *'I am planning to work on my dissertation at 5.30 p.m. this
> evening in my study, but I think it is unlikely that I will get
> down to doing any work on it.'*

Thus, it is likely that Harvey's UNE in this specific example is anxiety.

Common unhealthy negative emotions

There are times, however, when you may disturb yourself about other
adversities that do not appear in your formulated problems. In such
circumstances, you need to start from the beginning in identifying
the main unhealthy negative emotion that you experienced in this
situation. As before, you need to be specific in identifying your UNE,
since doing so will help you to identify the other elements in the
'Situational ABC' framework. The following list outlines the main
UNEs for which people seek help: anxiety, depression, guilt, shame,
hurt, unhealthy anger, unhealthy jealousy and unhealthy envy.

Try to identify your major UNE from the above list and avoid vague
statements of emotion such as 'I felt bad' or 'I felt upset'. Also avoid
using terms that are really adversities at 'A' such as 'I felt rejected'
and 'I felt criticized'.

What if you have more than one UNE in the situation?

You can experience more than one unhealthy negative emotion in
any given situation. Thus, imagine that your boss has asked you to

do a presentation at short notice. You may feel anxious and unhealthily angry about this. You may feel anxious about giving a poor presentation and unhealthily angry with your boss for putting you on the spot at short notice.

In such situations, choose the UNE that represents your biggest problem and work with that one first. However, at this point, what is more important is once you have chosen one UNE that you stick with this problem until you have dealt with it before switching to the other problem.

The difference between healthy and unhealthy negative emotions
You may be uncertain whether the negative emotion that you experienced in your selected example was unhealthy or healthy. If you misunderstand the difference between the two, you may try to change a healthy negative emotion.

There are three major ways of distinguishing between unhealthy and healthy negative emotions:

1 UNEs stem from irrational beliefs, while HNEs stem from rational beliefs.
2 UNEs are associated with behaviours that are dysfunctional, while HNEs are associated with behaviours that are functional.
3 UNEs are associated with thinking that is highly unrealistic and skewed to the negative, while HNEs are associated with thinking that is realistic and balanced.

Once you have identified your major UNE, write it on the form (see Appendix 1) next to 'C (emotional consequence)'.

IDENTIFY YOUR DYSFUNCTIONAL BEHAVIOUR

As I pointed out above, when you experience an unhealthy negative emotion, your associated behaviour is likely to be dysfunctional and as such it will make your emotional problem worse. As I pointed out in Chapter 2, there are two types of behaviour that you need to identify at 'C':

1 actual behaviours that are observable and
2 action tendencies where you 'feel like' acting in a certain way, but do not.

There are certain forms of behaviour that are frequently associated with particular unhealthy negative emotions. I provided a representative list in Table 1.2, but of course your job is to detail how you acted in the situation or what you 'felt like' doing, but did not do. Write this on the form next to 'C (behavioural consequence)'.

The case of Harvey

Harvey procrastinated on starting his dissertation and this was the behaviour that he wrote down on the form under 'C (behavioural consequence)'.

IDENTIFY YOUR SUBSEQUENT DISTORTED THINKING

When you feel an unhealthy negative emotion and act in a dysfunctional way at 'C', you also tend to think in ways that are highly distorted and exaggerated. I call this thinking 'subsequent distorted thinking' because it stems from irrational beliefs and because it is distorted in nature. There are certain forms of thinking that are frequently associated with particular unhealthy negative emotions. I provide a representative list in Table 6.1, but again your job is to identify your subsequent thinking in the example situation that you are assessing and write it on the form next to 'C (thinking consequence)'.

Table 6.1 Unhealthy negative emotions and illustrative subsequent distorted thinking.

Unhealthy negative emotion	Subsequent distorted thinking
Anxiety	Overestimating the negative consequences of the threat if it occurs
Depression	Hopelessness Helplessness
Guilt	Assigning too much responsibility to yourself and too little to others
Shame	Overestimating the negativity of others' reactions to yourself and the extent of these reactions

(Contd)

Unhealthy negative emotion	*Subsequent distorted thinking*
Hurt	Thinking that the other has to put things right of their own accord
Unhealthy anger	Thinking that the other has malicious intent Thoughts of exacting revenge
Unhealthy jealousy	Tending to see threats to your relationship in the absence of evidence
Unhealthy envy	Tending to denigrate the value of the desired possession

The case of Harvey

When he was anxious about beginning work on the dissertation his associated thought was: *'If I am not creative at the start, I never will be creative.'* This is an example of 'always and never' thinking which tends to stem from rigid and extreme beliefs. Harvey wrote this thought down under 'C (thinking consequence)' on his form (see Table 6.5).

Identify 'A'

You will recall that 'A' stands for 'adversity'. It represents what you were most disturbed about in the situation that provided the context for your emotional problem. While I suggested earlier that it might be useful to identify 'C' before 'A', these steps are, in fact, interchangeable and, if you prefer, you should identify 'A' before 'C'.

CONSULT YOUR FORMULATED PROBLEM

In Chapter 4 I discussed how to identify your problems and goals. You will recall that I showed you how to formulate your problem using REBT theory as a guide. If you take your formulated problem together with the specific example of this problem which you are assessing, then it may well be that the 'A' in your specific example will be a specific representation of the more general 'A' in your formulated problem. Ask yourself a relevant question such as: Is what I am most disturbed about in this specific example the same as what I am disturbed about in my formulated problem?

Let me show you what I mean by considering the case of Harvey. I have italicized the relevant points.

The case of Harvey

Harvey's formulated problem was as follows:

> *'Any time I plan to start work on my dissertation, I think that the work that I will do on it won't be very creative. I feel anxious about this, put off starting work on it and think that I will fail my dissertation and will end up on skid row.'*

Harvey's specific example of this problem was as follows:

> *'I have made plans to work on my dissertation at 5.30 p.m. tonight in my study, but it is unlikely that I will do so.'*

He then asked himself the question: *Is the reason I am likely to put off working tonight that I think that my work won't be creative?* His answer was that it was and this became his 'A'.

IDENTIFYING THE SPECIFIC EXAMPLE OF THE THEME

When you are endeavouring to identify your 'A', you might find it helpful to consult Table 1.1. This table lists the common inferential themes associated with the eight major unhealthy negative emotions. What you do is this:

▶ Use your major UNE at 'C' to identify your general theme (e.g. threat in anxiety) at 'A'.
▶ Ask yourself the following question (the content will vary according to the general theme at 'A' and your major UNE at 'C'): What did I find most threatening in this situation?
▶ The answer is probably your specific 'A' in your chosen example.

The case of Harvey

Harvey took his UNE at 'C' to identify the general theme of threat. He then asked himself: *In the situation where I have made plans to*
(Contd)

work on my dissertation at 5.30 p.m. tonight in my study, what am I likely to find most threatening in this situation so that I don't start on it? Harvey responded with the inference that his work may not be very creative.

USING THE 'MAGIC QUESTION'

When you use the 'magic question' technique to identify your 'A', you do the following:

▶ Focus on the 'situation' that you have described.
▶ Ask yourself what one thing would get rid of or significantly diminish the unhealthy negative emotion that you felt at 'C'.
▶ The opposite to this is your 'A'.

Insight

If you identify accurately what you are most disturbed about at 'A', it's like hitting the bull's eye in darts.

The case of Harvey

Here is how Harvey used the 'magic question' technique to identify his 'A' in his selected example.

▶ Focus on the 'situation' that you have described = *'I have made plans to work on my dissertation at 5.30 p.m. tonight in my study, but it is unlikely that I will do so because I will feel anxious when I think about starting.'*
▶ Ask yourself what one thing would get rid of or significantly diminish the anxiety that you felt at 'C' = *'My work being creative.'*
▶ The opposite to this is your 'A' = *'My work not being creative.'*

ASSUME TEMPORARILY THAT 'A' IS TRUE

Once you have identified your adversity at 'A', you may discover that it represents a clear distortion of reality. If this is the case, you may be tempted to question 'A'. Resist this temptation. Rather, at this stage you should assume temporarily that 'A' is correct. For example, in Harvey's case, it is not important to determine whether his work will be immediately creative. What is important is that he assumes temporarily that it won't be (i.e. that his 'A' is correct) in order to help himself to identify more accurately the irrational beliefs about the 'A' that led to his feelings at 'C'.

Later, you will have an opportunity to check whether your 'A' is likely to have been true (see Chapter 10).

Set emotional, behavioural and thinking goals

At some point in working with your specific example of your target problem, it is important to set goals with respect to the example. Here, realize that you will only be changing your responses to your adversity at 'A' and not the adversity itself. The whole point of what you are doing here is to help you to respond healthily to adversities. When you do so, you will be in a better frame of mind to attempt to change or realistically reinterpret 'A' than if you tried to do these things when you were disturbed about 'A'.

SET YOUR EMOTIONAL GOAL

When you set emotional goals, bear in mind that you will be selecting a healthy negative emotion. The emotion will be negative because your adversity is negative, but it will be healthy. In Chapter 2 I discussed the healthy alternatives to unhealthy negative emotions and these are presented below. However, as I have previously mentioned, it is important that you use your own term for the relevant healthy emotion rather than the one listed: concern (rather than anxiety), sadness (rather than depression), remorse (rather than guilt), disappointment (rather than shame), sorrow (rather than hurt), healthy anger (rather than unhealthy anger), healthy jealousy (rather than unhealthy jealousy), healthy envy (rather than unhealthy envy)... .

The case of Harvey

Harvey was anxious about not being creative if he were to start his dissertation, so he set as his emotional goal being concerned but not anxious about not being creative. He put *'concern'* under the heading 'C (emotional goal)' on his form (see Table 6.5).

SET YOUR BEHAVIOURAL GOAL

When you experience a healthy negative emotion, your associated behaviour is likely to be functional and as such it will help you to overcome your emotional problem. Your functional behavioural goal will be the opposite of your dysfunctional behaviour. As with dysfunctional behaviour, functional behaviour can be overt or an action tendency.

There are certain forms of behaviour that are frequently associated with particular healthy negative emotions. I provided a representative list in Table 1.2, but your job is to identify the healthy alternatives to your unhealthy behaviour. When you have done so, write this on the form next to 'C (behavioural goal)'.

The case of Harvey

Harvey's dysfunctional behaviour was *procrastination* on his dissertation. The healthy alternative to this (and also its opposite) is *'starting to work on the dissertation'*, which Harvey set as his behavioural goal (see Table 6.5).

SET YOUR THINKING GOAL

When you feel a healthy negative emotion and act in a functional way at 'C', you also tend to think in ways that are realistic and balanced in nature. I call this thinking 'subsequent realistic thinking' because it stems from rational beliefs and because it is realistic in nature. This thinking represents your thinking goal in the situation being assessed and should thus be placed under 'C (thinking goal)' on the form. It is a direct realistic and balanced alternative to the subsequent distorted thinking that you wrote down under 'C (thinking consequence)'. There are certain forms of thinking that are frequently associated with particular healthy negative emotions. I provide a representative list in Table 6.2.

Table 6.2 *Healthy negative emotions and illustrative subsequent realistic and balanced thinking.*

Healthy negative emotion	Subsequent realistic and balanced thinking
Concern (rather than anxiety)	Being realistic about the negative consequences of the threat if it occurs

Healthy negative emotion	Subsequent realistic and balanced thinking
Sadness (rather than depression)	Able to see good things happening in the future as well as bad Able to see yourself taking steps to help yourself
Remorse (rather than guilt)	Assigning the appropriate amount of responsibility to yourself and to others
Disappointment (rather than shame)	Being realistic concerning the negativity of others' reactions to you and the extent of these reactions
Sorrow (rather than hurt)	Thinking that you can sort the issue out with the other rather than waiting for that person to put things right of their own accord
Healthy anger (rather than problematic anger)	Thinking that the other may have malicious intent but not necessarily so Thoughts of communicating your feelings to the other and how to do so
Healthy jealousy (rather than problematic jealousy)	Tending to see threats to your relationship only in the presence of evidence
Healthy envy (rather than problematic envy)	Tending to appreciate rather than denigrate the value of the desired possession

The case of Harvey

Harvey's realistic thinking goal was as follows: 'I may not be creative at the beginning, but that does not mean that I can't be creative later.' Such a thinking goal would logically stem from a rational belief which is flexible and would allow for Harvey to be non-creative at the beginning of his work and to be creative later. Harvey wrote down this thought under the heading 'C (thinking goal)' on his form (see Table 6.5).

Identify your irrational beliefs (iBs)

You have now identified the 'A' and 'C' components of the specific example of your target problem and relevant goals. The next step is to identify your irrational beliefs at 'B' that accounted for your responses at 'C' to the adversity at 'A'. You will recall from Chapter 2 that there are four irrational beliefs: one rigid belief and three extreme beliefs (see Table 6.3).

Table 6.3 Irrational beliefs.

Rigid belief	*'I / You / Life must...'*
	↓
Extreme awfulizing belief	*'It's awful that...'*
Extreme discomfort intolerance belief	*'I can't bear it...'*
Extreme depreciation belief (self, other, life)	*'I / You / Life is no good...'*

In order to identify your irrational beliefs I suggest that you do the following:

▶ Take your 'A'.
▶ Identify the rigid belief that you held about 'A'.
▶ Identify the main extreme belief that you held about 'A'.
▶ Put all this information together.

(This is your composite irrational belief which you write down under the heading 'iB' – irrational belief – on the form in Appendix 1.)

Let me illustrate this in the case of Harvey.

The case of Harvey

▶ Take your 'A' = *What I do will not be creative.*
▶ Identify the rigid belief that you held about 'A' = *I must be creative.*

▶ Identify the main extreme belief that you held about 'A' = *If I am not creative, I am stupid.* This is what Harvey wrote down under the heading 'iB (irrational belief)' in the form (see Table 6.5).

▶ Put all this information together = *I must be creative and, if I'm not, I'm stupid.*

Identify the alternative rational beliefs (rBs)

The final step is for you to identify the rational beliefs that are the healthy alternatives to your already identified irrational beliefs. These beliefs will enable you to achieve your emotional, behavioural and thinking goals that you have listed on the right-hand side of the form. As we saw in Chapter 2, there are four irrational beliefs: one flexible belief and three non-extreme beliefs (see Table 6.4).

Table 6.4 Rational beliefs.

Flexible belief	*'It would be preferable if I / You / Life..., but it is not necessary...'*
Non-extreme non-awfulizing belief	*'It's bad, but not terrible that...'*
Non-extreme discomfort tolerance belief	*'It's hard, but I can bear it and it is worth it to me to do so...'*
Non-extreme acceptance belief (self, other, life)	*'I / You / Life is complex and too complex to be given a single rating...'*

In order to identify your alternative rational belief, you provide the flexible alternative to your rigid belief and the non-extreme alternative to your major extreme belief and then combine them. Then, you write this down on the 'Situational ABC' form (in Appendix 1) under the heading 'rB (rational belief)'.

Insight

It is easy to forget that beliefs determine whether we respond healthily or unhealthily to adversities. It is worthwhile reminding yourself of this from time to time.

Let me illustrate this with reference to the case of Harvey.

Here is how Harvey identified his rational belief by following the above guidelines:

Harvey's rigid belief *'I must be creative.'*	Harvey's flexible belief *'I would like to be creative, but I don't have to be.'*
Harvey's extreme self-depreciation belief *'If I am not creative, I am stupid.'*	Harvey's non-extreme self-acceptance belief *'If I am not creative, I am fallible, not stupid.'*
Harvey's irrational belief *'I must be creative and if I am not, I am stupid.'*	Harvey's rational belief *'I would like to be creative, but I don't have to be. If I am not creative, I am fallible not stupid.'*

I present Harvey's completed 'Situational ABC' form in Table 6.5.

Table 6.5 Harvey's 'Situational ABC' form without instructions.

'Situation' =	*I have made plans to work on my dissertation at 5.30 p.m. tonight in my study, but it is unlikely that I will do so.*
'A' =	*What I do will not be creative.*
'iB' (irrational belief) =	**'rB' (rational belief) =**
I must be creative and, if I am not, I am stupid.	*I would like to be creative, but I don't have to be. If I am not creative, I am fallible not stupid.*
'C' (emotional consequence) =	**'C' (emotional goal) =**
Anxiety	*Concern*

'C' (behavioural consequence) =	'C' (behavioural goal) =
Procrastination	*Start working on dissertation*
'C' (thinking consequence) =	'C' (thinking goal) =
If I am not creative at the start, I never will be creative.	*I may not be creative at the beginning, but that does not mean that I can't be creative later.*

THINGS TO REMEMBER

▶ Describe the situation in which you disturbed yourself as clearly and concretely as possible.

▶ When identifying your unhealthy negative emotion at 'C', consult your formulated problem or the list of UNEs in Chapter 1.

▶ If you are unsure whether your emotional 'C' is unhealthy or healthy, consider your beliefs, behaviour and subsequent thinking for clues.

▶ When identifying your dysfunctional behaviour at 'C', remember that this may be an overt behaviour or an action tendency.

▶ When identifying your dysfunctional thinking at 'C', remember that such thinking is likely to be highly distorted and skewed to the negative.

▶ When identifying what you are most disturbed about at 'A', consult your formulated problem, identify the theme associated with your unhealthy negative emotion and link this with the specific representation of this theme, or use the 'magic question' technique.

▶ Assume temporarily that your 'A' is true, since doing so will help you to identify your irrational beliefs. Resist the temptation to correct any distortions at 'A'. You will have an opportunity to do this later in the process.

▶ Don't forget to set emotional, behavioural and thinking goals with respect to the specific example of your target problem.

▶ Finally, identify the irrational beliefs (rigid and extreme beliefs) that underpin your disturbed response and the rational beliefs (flexible and non-extreme beliefs) that underpin your goals.

7

Focusing on and questioning your beliefs

In this chapter you will learn:
- *the purpose of questioning your irrational and rational beliefs*
- *the three main questions when questioning your irrational and rational beliefs*
- *the order I recommend you use when you question your beliefs.*

The main point of Cognitive Behaviour Therapy is that your emotions and behaviours are largely determined by the way you think about events rather than by the events themselves. In particular, Rational Emotive Behaviour Therapy, on which this book is based and which was the first approach to CBT to appear, holds that of all the thoughts we have about events it is our beliefs that largely determine our responses to these events.

In the previous chapter I showed you how to assess a specific example of your target problem and set appropriate emotional, behavioural and thinking goals. These goals are best achieved when you hold rational rather than irrational beliefs about the adversity in question at 'A'.

I showed you in the previous chapter how to identify your irrational beliefs and their rational alternatives. In this chapter I will discuss and illustrate how you can stand back and evaluate both of these beliefs so that you can commit yourself to strengthening your rational beliefs and weakening your irrational beliefs (see Chapter 8).

I am going to deal with rigid and flexible beliefs separately from extreme and non-extreme beliefs and when I consider the latter I will do so one at a time.

Questioning your beliefs: general issues

When you question your beliefs, you need to keep the following general issues in mind:

1 The purpose of questioning your beliefs is to help you decide which beliefs you want to operate on in future. In doing so, you need to ask yourself a number of questions:
   ▷ which belief is true and which is false and specify the reasons why
   ▷ which belief is sensible and which is illogical and the reasons why
   ▷ which belief has the healthiest consequences for you and which has the unhealthiest consequences and why.
2 You need to question both your irrational beliefs and your rational beliefs. If you only question your irrational beliefs you may understand that they are false, illogical and unhealthy, but you may not automatically see that your alternative rational beliefs are true, logical and healthy. You may only see this if you question your rational beliefs in the same way as you questioned your irrational beliefs.

> **Insight**
> Questioning both your irrational and rational beliefs helps you to understand with greater clarity why your irrational beliefs are irrational and why your rational beliefs are rational.

3 You can question your beliefs in a number of orders. Thus, you may question all your relevant irrational beliefs first before you question your alternative rational beliefs. In this book I advocate you questioning your rigid and flexible beliefs together and then your relevant extreme and non-extreme beliefs together. However, in doing so, I am not saying that this is the only order that you can employ to question your irrational and rational beliefs. If you find another order more useful, by all means employ it.
4 At the very least, I suggest that you question your rigid and flexible beliefs. If you do question your extreme and non-extreme

beliefs, you don't need to question all three. Preferably, you should question the main extreme belief that stems from your rigid belief and that best accounts for your disturbed emotion at 'C' and its non-extreme belief alternative.

Questioning your rigid and flexible beliefs

It is important to remember that at this point you are dealing with the specific rigid belief that you identified in Chapter 6 and its specific flexible alternative. I will deal with more general core beliefs in Chapter 11.

Here are the steps that I suggest you take while questioning your rigid and flexible beliefs.

1 Write down your rigid and flexible beliefs side by side on a piece of paper.
2 Ask yourself the following question: Which of these two beliefs is true and which is false? Give reasons for your answer. In Table 7.1 I provide suggestions to help you do this.
3 Ask yourself the following question: Which of these two beliefs is logical or sensible and which is illogical? Give reasons for your answer. In Table 7.1 I provide suggestions to help you do this.
4 Ask yourself the following question: Which of these two beliefs is most healthy for me and which is least healthy? Give reasons for your answer. In Table 7.1 I provide suggestions to help you do this.
5 On the basis of the above, you should now be in a position to commit yourself to strengthening your conviction in your flexible belief and to weakening your conviction in your rigid belief. I will deal with this issue more fully in the next chapter. If you have any remaining doubts about making this commitment, read Chapter 14. To put this commitment into practice, I suggest the first step is for you to write down the arguments that you find most persuasive which show why your rigid belief is irrational and why your flexible belief is rational.

Table 7.1 Reasons why rigid beliefs are false and illogical and have largely unhealthy consequences and why flexible beliefs are true and logical and have largely healthy consequences.

Rigid belief	Flexible belief
A rigid belief is false	**A flexible belief is true**
For such a demand to be true the demanded conditions would already have to exist when they do not. Or as soon as you make a demand then these demanded conditions would have to come into existence. Both positions are clearly false or inconsistent with reality.	A flexible belief is true because its two component parts are true. You can prove that you have a particular desire and can provide reasons why you want what you want. You can also prove that you do not have to get what you desire.
A rigid belief is illogical	**A flexible belief is logical**
A rigid belief is based on the same desire as a flexible but is transformed as follows:	A flexible belief is logical since both parts are not rigid and thus the second component logically follows from the first. Thus, consider the following flexible belief:
'I prefer that x happens (or does not happen) and therefore this absolutely must (or must not) happen.'	*'I prefer that x happens (or does not happen)...but this does not mean that it must (or must not) happen.'*
The first ('I prefer that x happens (or does not happen...)') is not rigid, but the second ('...and therefore this must (or must not) happen') is rigid. As such, a rigid belief is illogical since one cannot logically derive something rigid from something that is not rigid.	The first component ('I prefer that x happens (or does not happen...)') is not rigid and the second ('...but this does not mean that it must (or must not) happen') is also non-rigid. Thus, a flexible belief is logical because it comprises two non-rigid parts connected together logically.

Rigid belief	Flexible belief
A rigid belief has largely unhealthy consequences	**A flexible belief has largely healthy consequences**
A rigid belief has largely unhealthy consequences because it tends to lead to unhealthy negative emotions, unconstructive behaviour and highly distorted and biased subsequent thinking when the person is facing an adversity.	A flexible belief has largely healthy consequences because it tends to lead to healthy negative emotions, constructive behaviour, and realistic and balanced subsequent thinking when the person is facing an adversity.

Insight

For reasons of clarity, it is best to separate questioning your rigid and flexible beliefs from questioning your extreme and non-extreme beliefs.

The case of Harvey

You will remember Harvey from the previous chapter. Here I will show you how Harvey questioned his rigid and flexible beliefs by following the steps outlined above:

1 Harvey wrote down his rigid and flexible beliefs side by side on a piece of paper, thus:
   'I must be creative' v 'I would like to be creative, but I don't have to be.'
2 He then asked himself which of these beliefs was true and which was false. Here is what he said:
   'My rigid belief is false and my flexible belief is true. There is no reason why I have to be creative. If there was, there would be no chance that my work would not be creative. But there is such a chance. So my demand is untrue. Also, it would be very nice if my work would be creative if I held that demand, but it clearly isn't. In fact, when I hold that demand, I don't do any work! My flexible belief is true because there is evidence that I want to be creative and it is also true that I don't have to be creative.'
3 Harvey then asked himself which of these two beliefs was logical or sensible and which was illogical. Here is his answer:

(Contd)

'My rigid belief is illogical and my flexible belief is logical. My wish to be creative is, by itself, not rigid, but when I say that I have to be creative, I am converting that non-rigid idea into a rigid one for no logical reason. So, my demand is not logical. However, when I acknowledge that I don't have to be creative that is non-rigid and follows logically from my non-rigid idea that I would like to be creative. So my flexible belief is logical.'

4 Harvey then asked himself which of these two beliefs is most healthy for him and which is least healthy. Here is his answer: 'My rigid belief is unhealthy and my flexible belief is healthy. My rigid belief leads me to feel anxiety about starting my dissertation with the result that I put off working on it. By contrast, my flexible belief is much more helpful to me because it allows me to begin my dissertation even though I may not be creative. It allows me to develop creativity later rather than insisting that creativity be there from the outset.'

5 On the basis of the above, Harvey committed himself to strengthen his conviction in his flexible belief and to weaken his conviction in his rigid belief (see Chapter 8).

Harvey's only doubt about committing to his flexible belief at the expense of his rigid belief was that he thought that doing so meant that he would lower his standards about the creativity of his work. However, he realized that his flexible belief allowed him to retain his high standards but surrender his rigid idea about being creative. He also recognized that holding on to his rigid idea about being creative meant that, while he might maintain his high standards, he would not gain his degree because adhering to his rigid idea meant that he would not complete his dissertation. This latter argument was the one that Harvey found was most persuasive, so he wrote it down and resolved to review it several times a day and especially before beginning work on his dissertation.

I am now going to show you how to question your extreme beliefs and their non-extreme alternatives. As I do so, remember that I said that you do not have to question all three extreme and non-extreme beliefs. Rather, I suggested that you focus on the following:

▶ the one major extreme belief that, along with your rigid belief, in your view accounted for your disturbed feelings at 'C' and
▶ its non-extreme alternative.

Questioning your awfulizing and non-awfulizing beliefs

If you have chosen your awfulizing and non-awfulizing beliefs as the most relevant extreme and non-extreme beliefs to question, it is important to remember that you are dealing with the specific beliefs that you identified in Chapter 6. I will deal with more general core beliefs in Chapter 11.

Here are the steps that I suggest you take while questioning your awfulizing and non-awfulizing beliefs.

1 Write down your awfulizing and non-awfulizing beliefs side by side on a piece of paper.
2 Ask yourself the following question: Which of these two beliefs is true and which is false? Give reasons for your answer. In Table 7.2, I provide suggestions to help you do this.
3 Ask yourself the following question: Which of these two beliefs is logical or sensible and which is illogical? Give reasons for your answer. In Table 7.2 I provide suggestions to help you do this.
4 Ask yourself the following question: Which of these two beliefs is most healthy for me and which is least healthy? Give reasons for your answer. In Table 7.2 I provide suggestions to help you do this.
5 On the basis of the above, you should now be in a position to commit yourself to strengthening your conviction in your non-awfulizing belief and to weakening your conviction in your awfulizing belief. I will deal with this issue more fully in the next chapter. If you have any remaining doubts about making this commitment, read Chapter 14. To put this commitment into practice, I suggest the first step is for you to write down the arguments that most persuasively show why your awfulizing belief is irrational and why your non-awfulizing belief is rational.

Table 7.2 Reasons why awfulizing beliefs are false and illogical and have largely unhealthy consequences and why non-awfulizing beliefs are true and logical and have largely healthy consequences.

Awfulizing belief	Non-awfulizing belief
An awfulizing belief is false	**A non-awfulizing belief is true**
When you hold an awfulizing belief about your 'A', this belief is based on the following ideas:	When you hold a non-awfulizing belief about your 'A', this belief is based on the following ideas:
i) Nothing could be worse ii) The event in question is worse than 100 per cent bad iii) No good could possibly come from this bad event.	i) Things could always be worse ii) The event in question is less than 100 per cent bad iii) Good could come from this bad event.
All three ideas are patently false and thus your awfulizing belief is false.	All three ideas are clearly true and thus your non-awfulizing belief is true.
An awfulizing belief is illogical	**A non-awfulizing belief is logical**
An awfulizing belief is based on the same evaluation of badness as a non-awfulizing belief, but is transformed as follows:	A non-awfulizing belief is logical since both parts are non-rigid and thus the second component logically follows from the first. Thus, consider the following non-awfulizing belief:
'It is bad if x happens (or does not happen)…and therefore it is awful if it does happen (or does not happen).'	*'It is bad if x happens (or does not happen)… but it is not awful if x happens (or does not happen).'*
The first component ('It is bad if *x* happens (or does not happen…)') is non-extreme, but the second ('…and therefore it is awful if it does (or does not)	The first component ('It is bad if *x* happens (or does not happen…)') is non-extreme and the second ('…but it is not awful if it does (or does not

Awfulizing belief	Non-awfulizing belief
happen') is extreme. As such, an awfulizing belief is illogical since one cannot logically derive something extreme from something that is non-extreme.	happen)') is also non-extreme. Thus, a non-awfulizing belief is logical because it comprises two non-extreme parts connected together logically.
An awfulizing belief has largely unhealthy consequences	**A non-awfulizing belief has largely healthy consequences**
An awfulizing belief has largely unhealthy consequences because it tends to lead to unhealthy negative emotions, unconstructive behaviour and highly distorted and biased subsequent thinking when the person is facing an adversity.	A non-awfulizing belief has largely healthy consequences because it tends to lead to healthy negative emotions, constructive behaviour and realistic and balanced subsequent thinking when the person is facing an adversity.

Questioning your discomfort intolerance and discomfort tolerance beliefs

If you have chosen your discomfort intolerance and discomfort tolerance beliefs as the most relevant extreme and non-extreme beliefs to question, it is important to remember that you are dealing with the specific beliefs that you identified in Chapter 6. I will deal with more general core beliefs in Chapter 11.

Here are the steps that I suggest you take while questioning your discomfort intolerance and discomfort tolerance beliefs.

1 Write down your discomfort intolerance and discomfort tolerance beliefs side by side on a piece of paper.
2 Ask yourself the following question: Which of these two beliefs is true and which is false? Give reasons for your answer. In Table 7.3, I provide suggestions to help you do this.
3 Ask yourself the following question: Which of these two beliefs is logical or sensible and which is illogical? Give reasons for your answer. In Table 7.3, I provide suggestions to help you do this.

4 Ask yourself the following question: Which of these two beliefs is most healthy for me and which is least healthy? Give reasons for your answer. In Table 7.3, I provide suggestions to help you do this.

5 On the basis of the above, you should now be in a position to commit yourself to strengthening your conviction in your discomfort tolerance belief and to weakening your conviction in your discomfort intolerance belief. I will deal with this issue more fully in the next chapter. If you have any remaining doubts about making this commitment, read Chapter 14. To put this commitment into practice, I suggest the first step is for you to write down the arguments that you find most persuasive which show why your discomfort intolerance belief is irrational and why your discomfort tolerance belief is rational.

Table 7.3 Reasons why discomfort intolerance beliefs are false and illogical and have largely unhealthy consequences and why discomfort tolerance beliefs are true and logical and have largely healthy consequences.

Discomfort intolerance belief	Discomfort tolerance belief
A discomfort intolerance belief is false	**A discomfort tolerance belief is true**
When you hold a discomfort intolerance belief about your	When you hold a discomfort tolerance belief about your
'A', this belief is based on the following ideas which are all false:	'A', this belief is based on the following ideas which are all true:
i) I will die or disintegrate if the discomfort continues to exist.	i) I will struggle if the discomfort continues to exist, but I will neither die nor disintegrate.
ii) I will lose the capacity to experience happiness if the discomfort continues to exist.	ii) I will not lose the capacity to experience happiness if the discomfort continues to exist, although this capacity will be temporarily diminished.
iii) Even if I could tolerate it, the discomfort is not worth tolerating.	iii) The discomfort is worth tolerating.

All three ideas are patently false and thus your discomfort intolerance belief is false.	All three ideas are patently true and thus your discomfort tolerance belief is true.

A discomfort intolerance belief is illogical

A discomfort tolerance belief is logical

A discomfort intolerance belief is based on the same sense of struggle as a discomfort tolerance belief, but is transformed as follows:	A discomfort tolerance belief is logical since both parts are non-extreme and thus the second component logically follows from the first. Thus, consider the following discomfort tolerance belief:

'It would be difficult for me to tolerate it if x happens (or does not happen)…and therefore it would be intolerable.'	*'It would be difficult for me to tolerate it if x happens (or does not happen)…but it would not be intolerable (and it would be worth tolerating).'*

The first component ('It would be difficult for me to tolerate it if x happens (or does not happen…)') is non-extreme, but the second ('…and therefore it would be intolerable') is extreme. As such, a discomfort intolerance belief is illogical since one cannot logically derive something extreme from something that is non-extreme.	The first component ('It would be difficult for me to tolerate it if x happens (or does not happen…)') is non-extreme and the second ('…but it would not be intolerable (and it would be worth tolerating)') is also non-extreme. Thus, a discomfort tolerance belief is logical because it comprises two non-extreme parts connected together logically.

A discomfort intolerance belief has largely unhealthy consequences

A discomfort tolerance belief has largely healthy consequences

A discomfort intolerance belief has largely unhealthy consequences because it tends	A discomfort tolerance belief has largely healthy consequences because it tends

(Contd)

| --- | --- |
| to lead to unhealthy negative emotions, unconstructive behaviour, and highly distorted and biased subsequent thinking when the person is facing an adversity. | to lead to healthy negative emotions, constructive behaviour, and realistic and balanced subsequent thinking when the person is facing an adversity. |

Questioning your depreciation and acceptance beliefs

If you have chosen your depreciation and acceptance beliefs as the most relevant extreme and non-extreme beliefs to question, it is important to remember that you are dealing with the specific beliefs that you identified in Chapter 6. I will deal with more general core beliefs in Chapter 11.

Here are the steps that I suggest you take while questioning your depreciation and acceptance beliefs.

1 Write down your depreciation and acceptance beliefs side by side on a piece of paper.
2 Ask yourself the following question: Which of these two beliefs is true and which is false? Give reasons for your answer. In Table 7.4 I provide suggestions to help you do this.
3 Ask yourself the following question: Which of these two beliefs is logical or sensible and which is illogical? Give reasons for your answer. In Table 7.4 I provide suggestions to help you do this.
4 Ask yourself the following question: Which of these two beliefs is most healthy for me and which is least healthy? Give reasons for your answer. In Table 7.4, I provide suggestions to help you do this.
5 On the basis of the above, you should now be in a position to commit yourself to strengthening your conviction in your acceptance belief and to weakening your conviction in your depreciation belief. I will deal with this issue more fully in the next chapter. If you have any remaining doubts about making this commitment, read Chapter 14. To put this commitment into practice, I suggest the first step is for you to write down the arguments that you find most persuasive which show why your depreciation belief is irrational and why your acceptance belief is rational.

Table 7.4 Reasons why depreciation beliefs are false and illogical and have largely unhealthy consequences and why acceptance beliefs are true and logical and have largely healthy consequences.

Depreciation belief	Acceptance belief

A depreciation belief is false

When you hold a depreciation belief in the face of your 'A', this belief is based on the following ideas which are both false:

i) A person (self or other) or life can legitimately be given a single global rating that defines their or its essence and the worth of a person or of life is dependent upon conditions that change (e.g. my worth goes up when I do well and goes down when I don't do well).

ii) A person or life can be rated on the basis of one of his or her or its aspects.

Both of these ideas are patently false and thus your depreciation belief is false.

A depreciation belief is illogical

A depreciation belief is based on the idea that the whole of a person or of life can logically be defined by one of their or its parts. Thus:

An acceptance belief is true

When you hold an acceptance belief in the face of your 'A', this belief is based on the following ideas which are both true:

i) A person (self or other) or life cannot legitimately be given a single global rating that defines their or its essence and their or its worth, as far as they or it have it, is not dependent upon conditions that change (e.g. my worth stays the same whether or not I do well).

ii) Discrete aspects of a person, and life, can be legitimately rated, but a person or life cannot be legitimately rated on the basis of these discrete aspects.

Both of these ideas are patently true and thus your depreciation belief is true.

An acceptance belief is logical

An acceptance belief is based on the idea that the whole of a person or of life cannot be defined by one or more of their or its parts. Thus:

(Contd)

Depreciation belief	Acceptance belief
'X is bad...and therefore I am bad.'	'X is bad, but this does not mean that I am bad; I am a fallible human being even though x happened.'
This is known as the part–whole error, which is illogical.	Here the part–whole illogical error is avoided. Rather it is held that the whole incorporates the part which is logical.
A depreciation belief has largely unhealthy consequences	**An acceptance belief has largely healthy consequences**
A depreciation belief has largely unhealthy consequences because it tends to lead to unhealthy negative emotions, unconstructive behaviour, and highly distorted and biased subsequent thinking when the person is facing an adversity.	An acceptance belief has largely healthy consequences because it tends to lead to healthy negative emotions, constructive behaviour, and realistic and balanced subsequent thinking when the person is facing an adversity.

Insight

As you probably don't have time to question all your relevant extreme and non-extreme beliefs, select the pair that best accounts for your disturbed reaction and healthy alternative.

The case of Harvey

Here I will show you how Harvey questioned his self-depreciation and self-acceptance beliefs by following the steps outlined above.

1 Harvey wrote down self-depreciation and self-acceptance beliefs side by side on a piece of paper, thus:
   'If I am not creative, I am stupid' v 'If I am not creative, I am fallible, not stupid.'
2 He then asked himself which of these beliefs was true and which was false. Here is what he said:
   'My self-depreciation belief is false and my self-acceptance belief is true. If I were stupid, then I could only do stupid things. This is patently not true. On the other hand I can prove

that I am fallible and my lack of creativity is evidence of my
fallibility and not of my stupidity.'

3 Harvey then asked himself which of these two beliefs was logical
   or sensible and which was illogical. Here is his answer.
   'My self-depreciation is illogical and my self-acceptance
   is logical. My lack of creativity when I begin work on my
   dissertation is a small aspect of myself. When I say that I am
   stupid for not being creative, I am saying that the whole of
   myself is defined by this part of myself. This is known as the
   part–whole error. However, when I say that this is evidence of
   my fallibility (where I can do things well and make mistakes),
   I am saying that the whole of me contains this part, but is not
   defined by it.'

4 Harvey then asked himself which of these two beliefs is most
   healthy for him and which is least healthy. Here is his answer.
   'My self-depreciation belief is unhealthy and my self-acceptance
   belief is healthy. My self-depreciation belief leads me to feel
   anxiety about starting my dissertation with the result that
   I put off working on it. By contrast, my self-acceptance belief
   is much more helpful to me because it allows me to begin my
   dissertation even though I may not be creative. It allows me to
   develop creativity later rather than insisting that creativity be
   there from the outset.'

5 On the basis of the above, Harvey committed himself to strengthen
   his conviction in his self-acceptance belief and to weaken his
   conviction in his self-depreciation belief (see Chapter 8).

Harvey's only doubt about committing to his self-acceptance at the
expense of his self-depreciation was that he thought that doing so
meant that he would not wish to change. He then saw that he was
confusing self-acceptance with self-resignation and that in reality
self-acceptance does not preclude evaluating lack of creativity
negatively and wanting to work towards being more creative. The idea
that he could accept himself for not being creative and at the same time
work towards being more creative was a very persuasive argument for
Harvey and helped him to begin work on his dissertation.

In the next chapter I will discuss a number of methods that you can
use to begin to strengthen your conviction in your rational beliefs and
to weaken your conviction in your irrational beliefs.

THINGS TO REMEMBER

▶ Questioning your beliefs is the heart of the change process in REBT.

▶ When you question your rational and irrational beliefs, it is best to do so at the same time to help you see more clearly the differences between them.

▶ Question your rigid and flexible beliefs separately from your extreme and non-extreme beliefs.

▶ Get in the habit of always questioning your rigid and flexible beliefs and at least your most relevant extreme and non-extreme beliefs.

▶ When questioning your beliefs, ask about their validity (true or false), logical status (sensible or nonsensical) and pragmatic value (constructive or unconstructive).

▶ Continue the questioning process until you can acknowledge that your irrational beliefs are irrational (i.e. false, illogical and unconstructive) and your rational beliefs are rational (i.e. true, logical and constructive).

8

Strengthening your conviction in your rational beliefs

In this chapter you will learn:
- *the difference between intellectual insight and emotional insight*
- *five techniques designed to strengthen your conviction in your rational beliefs.*

Rational and irrational beliefs exert a huge influence on us, and having rational beliefs can make a real difference to the way that we feel and how we act. I present in this chapter a series of techniques designed to help you give more conviction and credence to your rational beliefs and to reduce your conviction in, and reliance on, your irrational beliefs. This is necessary because simply understanding intellectually that your rational beliefs are true, logical and helpful is not enough to effect change. This type of understanding is known as **intellectual insight**. If you have such insight you may say, for instance, 'Although I *understand* why my belief is rational, I don't yet *believe* it', or you may point to your head and say, 'Although I understand that my rational belief is rational up here,' while you point towards your gut and say, 'I don't feel it down here.'

Although intellectual insight is required to help you change particular rational beliefs, intellectual insight alone is not enough. The kind of insight you will need to promote change is known by REBT therapists as **emotional insight**. With this kind of insight you may say things like 'I don't just believe it in my head, but feel it in my gut' and 'I genuinely believe in my heart that my rational belief is true, logical and helpful.' But the true test of whether you have emotional insight into your rational beliefs is when your conviction in your rational beliefs leads to healthy emotions, functional (as opposed to dysfunctional) behaviour and, subsequently, realistic and balanced thinking.

In the next sections you will find techniques to help you believe at the gut level what you understand intellectually. My aim is to illustrate, rather than to be comprehensive in my coverage of these techniques.

The attack–response method

You can strengthen your conviction in a rational belief by responding persuasively to any attacks on such a belief, and the attack–response method is based on this idea.

INSTRUCTIONS ON HOW TO USE THE ATTACK–RESPONSE METHOD

Write down on a sheet of paper one of your rational beliefs (e.g. 'I would like to be creative, but I don't have to be. If I'm not creative, I am fallible, not stupid').

- ▶ On a percentage scale assess your present level of conviction in this belief, with 0 per cent = no conviction and 100 per cent = total conviction (i.e. 'I believe this in my gut and it strongly influences my feelings and my behaviour'). Under your belief write down this rating.
- ▶ Think of ways in which this rational belief could be *attacked* and write these down. Such an attack may be, for instance, a doubt, reservation or objection to this rational belief. The attack should also include an explicit irrational belief – for example:
  - ▷ *demand* – where you demand that you must get what you want or must not get what you don't want
  - ▷ *awfulizing belief* – in which you evaluate not getting what you demand as being the end of the world
  - ▷ *discomfort intolerance belief* – reflecting the idea that you can't bear the adversity that you are facing
  - ▷ *depreciation belief* – in which, for instance, you believe that any failure to fulfil your desire proves that you are worthless.
- ▶ Make this attack as genuine as you can. The more it reflects what you believe, the better.

▶ Respond to this attack as fully, persuasively and wholeheartedly as possible. It is vital that you respond to each part of the attack. In particular, do all you can to respond to irrational belief statements and to distorted or unrealistic inferences expressed in the form of a doubt, reservation or objection to the rational belief. Do this as persuasively as you can and note down your response.

▶ Continue until you have responded to each one of your attacks and until you are unable to come up with any more. Ensure throughout that you maintain your focus on the rational belief that you are aiming to reinforce.

This is not an easy exercise to do, and you may find it helpful to make the initial attacks fairly gentle to start with. After that, as your responses to the attacks improve, you can start to make the attacks more powerful and gradually increase the strength of your attacks. As you make an attack, try to do so in a way that convinces you of its reality. Then, in responding to the attack, do your best to destroy the attack and to reinforce your conviction in your rational belief.

Remember that the aim of this exercise is to strengthen your conviction in your rational belief, so you should only regard the exercise as finished when you have responded to all of your attacks.

When you have responded to all the attacks, revise your ratings of your level of conviction in your rational belief using the 0–100 per cent scale as previously. If you have replied persuasively to your attacks, this rating will have improved markedly.

....

Insight

The attack–response technique is based on the principle of judo where you strengthen your conviction in your rational beliefs by responding to reasonable attacks on them.

....

The case of Harvey

Here is how Harvey used the attack–response method:

> **Rational belief:** *'I would like to be creative, but I don't have to be. If I am not creative, I am fallible not stupid.'*
>
> *Conviction rating of rational belief = 30%*
>
> *(Contd)*

Attack: But that's a cop-out. Creative people are intelligent and non-creative people are stupid – end of!

Response: Wait a minute! I am talking as if people can be divided into two types: creative people and non-creative people. In reality, the situation is much more complicated than that. There are only people who at times can be creative and at other times non-creative. If I begin my work and it's not creative, I can always be creative later. My creativity at any point in time does not transform me into being a creative, intelligent person just as my non-creativity does not transform me into being a non-creative stupid person. My identity does not change if I start off by being non-creative on my dissertation and then when I get into it by being creative. I am the same person in both cases; the only thing that changes is the creativity or otherwise of my work.

Attack: But if I want to be creative, the best way of ensuring that I am is to demand it of myself.

Response: Well, if that was right, I would be working and my work would be creative right from the start. Actually, the opposite is the case. My demand that I have to be creative is leading me to put off working because I am so scared that my work won't be creative. In my case, creativity does not thrive on fear. The fear destroys it.

Conviction rating of original rational belief = 80%

There are several variations on the attack–response method. For instance, try recording the dialogue on a DVR (digital voice recorder), in which case you should ensure that your response is more forceful in language and tone than your attack.

Rational-emotive imagery

Rational-emotive imagery (REI) is a method of using imagery which is intended to help you practise changing a *specific* irrational belief to its healthy alternative while you focus your mind on what you are most disturbed about in the *particular* situation in which you felt disturbed. You can only use REI while imagining specific situations, and therefore you are advised to use it only to strengthen your conviction in *particular* rational beliefs.

REI hinges on the fact that imagery can be used to help you surmount your problems or, although unintentionally, to practise thinking unhealthily as you imagine a large number of negative situations about which you disturb yourself. In the case of such negative imagery, when you imagine a negative event and disturb yourself about it, you are likely to do so by contemplating the event in your mind's eye and unwittingly rehearsing irrational beliefs about the event. Thus, you may literally practise disturbing yourself and simultaneously strengthen your conviction in your irrational beliefs.

You can fortunately also use your imagination constructively. While imagining, for example, the same negative event, you can practise changing your unhealthy negative emotions to their healthy equivalents by transforming your particular irrational beliefs into particular rational beliefs.

INSTRUCTIONS ON HOW TO USE REI

▶ Think of a situation in which you disturbed yourself and identify the aspect of the situation that most disturbed you (e.g. imagine you are about to start work on your dissertation, but are aware that you are not in a very creative frame of mind).

▶ Close your eyes and imagine the situation as vividly as you can and focus on the worst aspect of the situation – the *adversity* at 'A' (the activating event).

▶ Let yourself really experience the unhealthy negative emotion that you felt at the time while still concentrating intently on the 'A'. Make sure that your unhealthy negative emotion is *one* of the following: anxiety, depression, shame, guilt, hurt, unhealthy anger, unhealthy jealousy, unhealthy envy.

▶ Genuinely experience this disturbed emotion for a short while (a few seconds) and then turn your emotional response to a healthy negative emotion, while simultaneously concentrating your mind on the adversity at 'A'. Do not change the intensity of the emotion, only the emotion. Therefore, if your original unhealthy negative emotion was anxiety, change it to concern; change your depression to sadness, shame to disappointment, guilt to remorse, hurt to sorrow, unhealthy anger to healthy anger, unhealthy jealousy to healthy jealousy and unhealthy envy to healthy envy. Thus you change the unhealthy negative emotion into its healthy equivalent, while ensuring that the level of intensity of the new emotion is as strong as the old emotion.

Keep experiencing this new emotion for about five minutes, all the time focusing on the adversity at 'A'. If you return to the old, unhealthy negative emotion, bring back the new healthy negative emotion.

▶ After five minutes, ask yourself how you changed your emotion.

▶ Ensure that you changed your emotional response by changing your specific irrational belief to its healthy equivalent. If you did not do so (if, for instance, you changed your emotion by changing the 'A' to make it less negative or neutral or by holding an indifference belief about the 'A'), redo the exercise and keep doing so until you have changed your emotion only by changing your specific unhealthy belief to its healthy equivalent.

▶ Practise REI several times a day, aiming for 30 minutes a day. You could practise it more often and for longer when you are about to face a negative situation about which you are likely to disturb yourself.

> **Insight**
>
> While you can plan times to practise REI, you can also use the technique at odd moments during the day such as waiting for a bus or standing in a queue.

The case of Harvey

This is how Harvey used REI. He imagined that he was about to start work on his dissertation but was aware that he was not in a very creative frame of mind. He focused on his lack of creativity and made himself feel anxious about this and felt life procrastination. Then, while still focusing on his lack of creativity, Harvey changed his feeling of anxiety to concern and saw himself begin work on his dissertation, even though he was not in a creative frame of mind. He checked that he had changed his irrational belief (i.e. '*I must be creative when I begin working on my dissertation*') to the corresponding rational belief (i.e. '*I would like to be creative when I begin working on my dissertation, but this state of mind is not necessary*') and, when he was satisfied that he had, he went back and focused on his rational beliefs for ten minutes. He practised REI formally three times a day, each time for ten minutes, but also did so 'on the hoof' as it were and snatched a few minutes' practice here and there during the day.

Teaching rational beliefs to others

You can also strengthen your conviction in your rational beliefs by teaching them to others. I am not advocating that you play the role of therapist to friends and relatives, nor that you foist these ideas on people who have no interest in discussing them. Instead, I am suggesting that you teach rational beliefs to those who hold the alternative irrational beliefs and are interested in hearing what you may have to say on the subject. In doing this, and particularly when someone argues with your viewpoint in defending their position, you will be able to get the experience of responding to their arguments with persuasive arguments of your own and thus strengthen your conviction in your own rational beliefs. Do this after having developed competence in using the written attack–response method discussed above, since the to-and-fro discussion which often follows when you try to teach rational beliefs to others is reminiscent of this technique.

The case of Harvey

Harvey knew a number of students who also believed that they had to be in a creative frame of mind before beginning academic work and in a one-to-one setting he endeavoured to teach them the REBT position on this irrational belief and the rational alternative to it. Through discussing this issue with his fellow students, Harvey was able to spot and respond to a number of rationalizations that he held to justify not beginning work on his dissertation such as:

Working when I am in a non-creative frame of mind taints the dissertation.

Response: *By holding this idea, I am thinking that my dissertation is like a sacred text which will be tainted by lack of creativity. It's a dissertation and not a sacred text and if I am not prepared to work while in a non-creative frame of mind then my sacred text will be full of blank pages!*

Working while in a non-creative frame of mind means that I am putting up with second best.

(Contd)

> *Response:* Well, even if it does mean this, I would still complete my dissertation and get my degree and I would rather do this and it not be top class than not get my degree at all. But even though I may start my work in a non-creative frame of mind, I may well get into a creative frame of mind as I get into the work. So, I am not necessarily settling for second best if I begin non-creatively.

Use rational self-statements

Having developed your rational beliefs, try developing shorthand versions of these beliefs which you can write down on a small card or type into your mobile phone so that you can review them later periodically. You will find such a review useful not only before you face an adversity but when you are actually facing it, assuming that you are able to glance at your rational message. You can also repeat these self-statements to yourself forcefully and persuasively. When you review or use such rational self-statements, focus hard on their meaning. Mere mindless repetition of these statements will have little or no impact on your feelings or behaviour.

The case of Harvey

Here are a few examples of rational self-statements that Harvey developed:

> 'Not being creative does not have to stop me from beginning work on my dissertation.'
> 'I am not stupid if I'm not creative; just fallible.'

Rehearse your rational beliefs while acting and thinking in ways that are consistent with these beliefs

Probably the most powerful method of reinforcing your rational belief is to rehearse it while you face the relevant adversity at 'A' and while you act and think in ways that chime with this rational belief. When your behaviour and thinking are working together and you keep them working together, you make the most of your chances of strengthening your conviction in your rational belief. You also need to refrain from acting and thinking in ways that follow your old irrational belief. It will be difficult for you to prevent yourself from doing so because you are used to acting and thinking in the old unreconstructed ways when your irrational belief is activated. Yet if you monitor your belief, behaviour and subsequent thinking, and respond constructively when you notice unhealthy instances of them, you will obtain valuable experience at strengthening your conviction in your rational belief.

As you work to reinforce your conviction in your rational beliefs, remember the following:

▶ You may have been using safety-seeking strategies to help you avoid facing adversities or to give you a feeling of comfort and security if you have to face these adversities. If you carry on employing these strategies while trying to change your irrational beliefs you will not change these beliefs. Identify how you use these strategies (which are largely behavioural and thinking-based in nature and can often be subtle and difficult to detect) and confront and dispute the irrational beliefs on which they are frequently based so that you can face the adversities fairly and squarely as you rehearse your developing rational beliefs.

▶ You will only experience emotional change (from negative and unhealthy to negative and healthy) after regular integrated practice in which you rehearse your rational belief and act and think in ways consistent with these beliefs. Changes in your emotions tend to lag behind behavioural change and thinking change. If you understand this, then you will keep on working to change your belief, behaviour and subsequent thinking and you will not be discouraged when your feelings take longer to change.

▶ If you wish to strengthen your conviction in your rational beliefs, you need to expose yourself to events that will challenge you, but which will not overwhelm you at that time. To make the most of such exposure, you must do it regularly while rehearsing your target rational belief and thinking realistically. As you progress, keep stretching yourself until you can face more and more challenging events.

The case of Harvey

Harvey strengthened his rational belief by rehearsing this belief
(i.e. *'I would like to be creative, but I don't have to be. If I am not
creative, I am fallible not stupid'*) while beginning work on his
dissertation at agreed times whether he was in a creative frame of
mind or not. While he did so, he briefly reminded himself that
while he might not be creative at the beginning of a work session,
he might get into a creative frame of mind later.

In the next chapter I will offer suggestions on how to deal with the
highly distorted negative thinking consequences of irrational beliefs.

THINGS TO REMEMBER

▶ Questioning your beliefs as described in Chapter 7 was designed to bring about intellectual insight into the irrationality of your irrational beliefs and the rationality of your rational beliefs. For you to strengthen your conviction in your rational beliefs you need to use more powerful and persuasive methods.

▶ If you repeatedly use the five methods described in this chapter then your conviction in your rational beliefs will increase, but only if you use them with spirit and energy.

▶ The most powerful way of strengthening your conviction in your rational beliefs is to act in ways that are consistent with them. When you do so, it is important that you remember that emotional change will initially lag behind behavioural change and thinking change, but will catch up if you persist in acting in ways that are in line with your rational beliefs.

9

Responding to highly distorted thoughts at 'C'

In this chapter you will learn:
* *how to recognize the thinking consequences of irrational beliefs*
* *that a variety of thinking errors stem from irrational beliefs*
* *that realistic and balanced thinking alternatives to these thinking errors stem from rational beliefs*
* *three ways of responding constructively to the thinking consequences of irrational beliefs.*

As you will now know, this book is based on the ideas of Rational Emotive Behaviour Therapy (REBT), one of the earliest forms of Cognitive Behaviour Therapy (CBT). The main idea that I have presented in this book so far is that you can use REBT's 'ABC' framework to make sense of your emotional problems and particular specific examples of these problems. You will recall that 'A' stands for adversity, 'B' stands for the beliefs that you hold about the adversity and 'C' stands for the consequences of these beliefs. There are three sets of such consequences: *emotional* consequences, *behavioural* consequences and *thinking* consequences.

When you hold irrational beliefs at 'B' about the adversity at 'A', your emotional consequences will be negative and unhealthy. I pointed out in Chapters 4 and 6 that your emotional goals in such circumstances are to experience emotions that are negative and healthy. You do this by changing your beliefs (from irrational to rational) and strengthen your rational beliefs as I described in the previous chapter. In that chapter I also showed that when you change your behavioural consequences (from unconstructive to constructive) you do so by formulating the opposite of your unconstructive behavioural response and by acting on the new response while rehearsing your rational belief. Thus, instead of avoiding an adversity that you find threatening (at 'A'), you face up to it while rehearsing your rational belief (at 'B').

In this chapter I am going to focus on the thinking consequences of your beliefs and in particular, I will show you how to recognize the thinking consequences of your irrational beliefs and how to respond to them.

How to recognize the thinking consequences of irrational beliefs

The thinking consequences of irrational beliefs (hereafter in this chapter referred to as TCs) are generally forms of thinking that you engage in once 'under the influence', so to speak, of your irrational beliefs. Here are some tips to help you to recognize them.

TCs ARE SKEWED TO THE NEGATIVE, HIGHLY DISTORTED AND LARGELY INFERENTIAL IN NATURE

When you focus on your adversity at 'A' and hold a set of irrational beliefs about this 'A' then the thinking consequences of these beliefs tend to be inferences. If you recall from Chapter 6, inferences are hunches about events that go beyond the data at hand. They may be correct or distorted and need to be tested against the available information. Inferences occur at 'A' in the 'ABC' and in TCs at 'C'. When these TCs stem from irrational beliefs, these inferences tend to be much more skewed to the negative and much more distorted than the inferences that occur at 'A'. Remember this point as you work to identify your TCs of irrational beliefs and when differentiating between inferences at 'A' and inferences at 'C'. This difference will become clearer when I discuss the case of Harvey.

Insight

The inferences that are the product of irrational beliefs are more distorted than the inferences at 'A' that trigger the irrational beliefs. This is because the former have been processed by irrational beliefs and the latter have not.

The case of Harvey

In the example of his problem that I discussed in Chapter 6 and which appears in Table 6.5, Harvey's 'A' was *'I might not be creative'*
(Contd)

and the TC of his irrational belief was *'If I am not creative at the start, I never will be creative.'* As you can see this latter inference is far more distorted than the inference at 'A'.

TCs ARE CHARACTERIZED BY A NUMBER OF THINKING ERRORS THAT ARE BASED ON IMPLICIT IRRATIONAL BELIEFS

Aaron T. Beck is the founder of Cognitive Therapy (CT), a form of CBT that first appeared in the 1970s and which is perhaps the predominant approach with the CBT tradition today. David Burns (1980), who wrote the first self-help book on Cognitive Therapy, outlined a number of thinking errors that are most often present in TCs. Let me outline and illustrate some of the most common thinking errors. As you will see, these TCs are highly distorted interpretations or inferences.

I will begin by describing each thinking error and then I will illustrate each error twice. First, I will illustrate the thinking error as it often appears in your thinking (i.e. without the underpinning irrational belief). Then, I illustrate and show how each error actually stems from an underlying irrational belief, which appears in square brackets in the second of the illustrations. In both illustrations I will underline the thinking error.

Let me reiterate that as the underlying irrational beliefs are implicit in your thinking, they may well not appear in your conscious thoughts and have to be looked for just beneath the surface of your conscious awareness.

Jumping to unwarranted conclusions
Description: Here, when something bad happens, you make a negative interpretation and treat this as a fact even though there is no definite evidence that convincingly supports your conclusions.

Illustration without irrational belief: 'Since they have seen me fail, they will view me as an incompetent worm.'

Illustration with irrational belief: 'Since they have seen me fail … [as I absolutely should not have done] … they will view me as an incompetent worm.'

All-or-none thinking
Description: Here, you use non-overlapping black and white categories.

Illustration without irrational belief: 'If I fail at any important task, <u>I will only ever fail again</u>.'

Illustration with irrational belief: 'If I fail at any important task... [as I must not do] ... <u>I will only ever fail again</u>.'

Overgeneralization
Description: Here, when something bad happens, you make a generalization from this experience that goes far beyond the data at hand.

Illustration without irrational belief: 'If my boss does not like me, <u>it follows that nobody at work will like me</u>.'

Illustration with irrational belief: '[My boss must like me.] If my boss does not like me, <u>it follows that nobody at work will like me</u>.'

Focusing on the negative
Description: Here, you pick out a single negative detail and dwell on it exclusively so that your vision of all reality becomes darkened, like the drop of ink that discolours the entire glass of water.

Illustration without irrational belief: 'As things are going wrong, <u>I can't see any good that is happening in my life</u>.'

Illustration with irrational belief: 'As things are going wrong ... [as they must not do and it is intolerable that they are] ... <u>I can't see any good that is happening in my life</u>.'

Disqualifying the positive
Description: Here, you reject positive experiences by insisting they 'don't count' for some reason or other, thus maintaining a negative view that cannot be contradicted by your everyday experiences.

Illustration without irrational belief: 'When others compliment me on the good things I have done, <u>they are only being kind to me by seeming to forget the foolish things I have done</u>.'

Illustration with irrational belief: '[I absolutely should not have done the foolish things that I have done]... When others compliment me on the good things I have done, <u>they are only being kind to me by seeming to forget those things</u>.'

Mind reading
Description: Here, you arbitrarily conclude that someone is reacting negatively to you, and you don't bother to check this out. You regard your thought as a fact.

Illustration without irrational belief: 'I made some errors in the PowerPoint presentation and, <u>when I looked at my boss, I thought he was thinking how hopeless I was and therefore he did think this</u>.'

Illustration with irrational belief: 'I made some errors in the PowerPoint presentation ... [that I absolutely should not have made] ... and <u>when I looked at my boss, I thought he was thinking how hopeless I was and therefore he did think this</u>.'

Fortune-telling
Description: Here, you anticipate that things will turn out badly, and you feel convinced that your prediction is an already established fact.

Illustration without irrational belief: 'Because I failed at this simple task, <u>I think that I will get a very bad appraisal and thus this will happen</u>.'

Illustration with irrational belief: 'Because I failed at this simple task ... [which I absolutely should not have done] ... <u>I think that I will get a very bad appraisal and thus this will happen</u>.'

Always-and-never thinking
Description: Here, when something bad happens, you conclude that it will always happen and/or the good alternative will never occur.

Illustration without irrational belief: 'Because my present conditions are not good, <u>they'll always be this way and I'll never have any happiness</u>.'

Illustration with irrational belief: 'Because my present conditions of living are not good ... [and they are actually intolerable because they must be better than they are] ... <u>it follows that they'll always be this way and I'll never have any happiness</u>.'

Magnification
Description: Here, when something bad happens, you exaggerate its negativity.

Illustration without irrational belief: 'I made a faux pas when introducing my new colleague <u>and this will have a very negative effect on my career</u>.'

Illustration with irrational belief: 'I made a faux pas when introducing my new colleague ... [which I absolutely should not have done and it's awful that I did so] ... <u>and this will have a very negative effect on my career</u>.'

Minimization
Description: Here you inappropriately shrink things until they appear tiny (your own desirable qualities or other people's imperfections).

Illustration without irrational belief: '<u>When I have seemingly done reasonably well, this is the result of luck and anyone could have done this. Whereas if another person had done the same thing, I would acknowledge their achievement</u>.'

Illustration with irrational belief: '[I must do outstandingly well and I am completely useless when I do not do so]... <u>When I have seemingly done reasonably well, this is the result of luck and anyone could have done this. Whereas if another person had done the same thing, I would acknowledge their achievement</u>.'

Emotional reasoning
Description: Here, you assume that your negative emotions necessarily reflect the way things really are: 'I feel it, therefore it must be true.'

Illustration without irrational belief: 'Because I have performed so poorly, <u>I feel like everybody will remember my poor performance and my strong feeling proves that they will</u>.'

Illustration with irrational belief: 'Because I have performed so poorly ... [as I absolutely should not have done] ... <u>I feel like everybody will remember my poor performance and my strong feeling proves that they will</u>.'

Personalization
Description: Here, when a negative event occurs involving you that you may or may not be primarily responsible for, you see yourself definitely as the cause of it.

Illustration without irrational belief: 'I am involved in a group presentation and things are not going well. As the audience is laughing, <u>I am sure they are laughing only at me</u>.'

Illustration with irrational belief: 'I am involved in a group presentation and things are not going well... [Since I am acting worse than I absolutely should act] ... and the audience is laughing, <u>I am sure they are laughing only at me</u>.'

Thus, if your thinking is highly distorted and skewed to the negative and falls under the heading of one (or more) of the above thinking errors, then this thinking is most likely a thinking consequence of your irrational belief as demonstrated in the second of the two presented illustrations.

> **Insight**
> Irrational beliefs are the breeding ground for a host of thinking errors.

The case of Harvey

Harvey identifies the thinking consequence of his irrational belief as: *'If I am not creative at the start, I never will be creative.'* This is clearly a thinking consequence as it is an example of the thinking error known as 'always-and-never thinking' and stems from an irrational belief – *'I must be creative at the start.'*

TCs ARE THOUGHTS THAT OFTEN ACCOMPANY UNHEALTHY NEGATIVE EMOTIONS THAT ARE PARTICULARLY RELEVANT TO THE ADVERSITY AT 'A'

When you are actually experiencing an unhealthy negative emotion (UNE) and you attend to the thinking that accompanies it, then these thoughts are likely to be TCs of irrational beliefs, the content of which is related to the adversity at 'A'. As they are TCs of irrational beliefs, this content is highly distorted and skewed to the negative.

The case of Harvey

When Harvey felt anxious about beginning work on his dissertation and paid attention to his accompanying thought that was related to his 'A' (i.e. the level of the creativity of his work), he identified this thought as: *'If I am not creative at the start, I never will be creative.'*

How to formulate realistic and balanced alternatives to thinking consequences of irrational beliefs

Before you respond to the thinking consequences of irrational beliefs, you need to formulate realistic alternatives to these TCs. The first step in doing this is to understand what are the realistic alternatives to the thinking errors listed and illustrated earlier in this chapter. The nature of these alternatives is that they are realistic (i.e. reflect accurately the nature of what has happened, is happening or may happen in the future) and they are balanced (i.e. they incorporate a variety of features – positive, negative and neutral). Table 9.1 provides such a handy list.

Table 9.1 Twelve thinking errors and their realistic and balanced alternatives.

Thinking error	Realistic and balanced alternative
Jumping to unwarranted conclusions	Sticking to the facts and testing out your hunches
All-or-none thinking	Multi-category thinking
Overgeneralization	Making a realistic generalization
Focusing on the negative	Focusing on the complexity of experiences
Disqualifying the positive	Incorporating the positive into a complex view of your experiences
Mind reading	Owning and checking one's thoughts about the reactions of others
Fortune-telling	Owning and checking one's thoughts about what will happen in the future
Always-and-never thinking	Balanced thinking about the past, present and future
Magnification	Keeping things in realistic perspective
Minimization	Using the same balanced perspective for self and others
Emotional reasoning	Sound reasoning based on thinking and feeling
Personalization	Making a realistic attribution

When I discussed the 'twelve thinking errors' earlier in this chapter, I emphasized the REBT view that these distortions tend to be underpinned by irrational beliefs. I exemplified this in the second of the two illustrations presented for each error. Inferences that are realistic and balanced in nature are also underpinned by beliefs, but these beliefs are rational in nature. As such, these realistic and balanced inferences can be viewed as thinking consequences of rational beliefs. In Table 9.2 I describe and illustrate both sets of thinking consequences (those reflecting thinking errors and those reflecting realistic and balanced thinking) and show how each are based on irrational and rational beliefs respectively.

Table 9.2 Descriptions, foundations and illustrations of thinking errors and their realistic and balanced alternatives.

Descriptions of thinking errors and realistic and balanced alternatives	Illustrations[1]
Jumping to unwarranted conclusions	
Here, when something bad happens, you make a negative interpretation and treat this as a fact even though there is no definite evidence that convincingly supports your conclusions.	'Since they have seen me fail … [as I absolutely should not have done] … <u>they will view me as an incompetent worm.</u>'
Sticking to the facts and testing out your hunches	
Here, when something bad happens, you stick to the facts and resolve to test out any negative interpretations you may make which you view as hunches to be examined rather than as facts.	'Since they have seen me fail … [as I would have preferred not to do, but do not demand that I absolutely should not have done] … I am not sure how they will view me. <u>I think that some will think badly of me, others will be compassionate</u>

Descriptions of thinking errors and realistic and balanced alternatives	Illustrations[1]
	towards me and yet others may not have noticed or be neutral about my failure. I can always ask them, if I want to know.'

All-or-none thinking

Here, you use non-overlapping black or white categories.

'If I fail at any important task ... [as I must not do] ... I will only ever fail again.'

Multi-category thinking

Here, you make use of a number of relevant categories.

'If I do fail at any important task ... [as I would prefer not to do, but do not demand that I must not do] ... I may well both succeed and fail at important tasks in the future.'

Overgeneralization

Here, when something bad happens, you make a generalization from this experience that goes far beyond the data at hand.

'[My boss must like me] ... If my boss does not like me, it follows that nobody at work will like me.'

Making a realistic generalization

Here, when something goes wrong, you make a generalization from this experience that is warranted by the data at hand.

'[I want my boss to like me, but he does not have to do so] ... If my boss does not like me, it follows that others at work may or may not like me.'

Focusing on the negative

Here, you pick out a single negative detail and dwell on it exclusively so that your

'As things are going wrong ... [as they must not do and it is intolerable that they are]

(Contd)

Descriptions of thinking errors and realistic and balanced alternatives	Illustrations[1]
vision of all reality becomes darkened, like the drop of ink that discolours the entire glass of water.	... <u>I can't see any good that is happening in my life.</u>'
Focusing on the complexity of experiences	
Here, you focus on a negative detail, but integrate this detail into the complexity of positive, negative and neutral features of life.	'As things are going wrong ... [as I prefer, but do not demand, that they must not and when they do, I can bear it] ... <u>I can see that my life is made up of the good, the bad and the neutral.</u>'
Disqualifying the positive	
Here, you reject positive experiences by insisting they 'don't count' for some reason or other, thus maintaining a negative view that cannot be contradicted by your everyday experiences.	'[I absolutely should not have done the foolish things that I have done] ... When others compliment me on the good things I have done, <u>they are only being kind to me by seeming to forget those foolish things.</u>'
Incorporating the positive into a complex view of your experiences	
Here, you accept positive experiences and incorporate these into the complexity of positive, negative and neutral features of life.	'[I would have preferred not to have done the foolish things that I have done, but that does not mean that I absolutely should not have done them] ... When others compliment me on the good things I have done, <u>I can accept these compliments as being genuine</u>

Descriptions of thinking errors and realistic and balanced alternatives	Illustrations[1]
	even though I also did some foolish things which the others may also have recognized.'

Mind reading

Here, you arbitrarily conclude that someone is reacting negatively to you, and you don't bother to check this out. You regard your thought as a fact.

'I made some errors in the PowerPoint presentation ... [that I absolutely should not have made] ... and when I looked at my boss, I thought he was thinking how hopeless I was and therefore he did think this.'

Owning and checking one's thoughts about the reactions of others

Here, you may think someone is reacting negatively to you, but you check it out with the other person rather than regarding your thought as fact.

'I made some errors in the PowerPoint presentation ... [that I would have preferred not to have made, but that does not mean that I absolutely should not have made them] ... and when I looked at my boss I thought he was thinking that I was hopeless, but I quickly realized that this was my thought rather than his and resolved to ask him about this in the morning.'

Fortune-telling

Here, you anticipate that things will turn out badly, and you feel convinced that your prediction is an already established fact.

'Because I failed at this simple task ... [which I absolutely should not have done] ... I think that I will get a very bad appraisal and thus this will happen.'

(Contd)

Descriptions of thinking errors and realistic and balanced alternatives	Illustrations[1]
Owning and checking one's thoughts about what will happen in the future	
Here, you anticipate that things may turn out badly, but you regard that as a prediction that needs examining against the available data and not as an established fact.	'Because I failed at this simple task ... [which I would have preferred not to have done, but do not have to be immune from so doing] ... <u>I may get a very bad appraisal, but this is unlikely since I have done far more good than bad at work during the last year.</u>'
Always-and-never thinking	
Here, when something bad happens, you conclude that it will always happen and/or the good alternative will never occur.	'Because my present conditions of living are not good ... [and they are actually intolerable because they must be better than they are] ... <u>it follows that they'll always be this way and I'll never have any happiness.</u>'
Balanced thinking about the past, present and future	
Here, when something bad happens, you recognize that while it may happen again it is not inevitable that it will and it is very unlikely that it will always occur. Also, you recognize that the good alternative may well occur in the future and that it is very unlikely that it will never happen.	'Because my present conditions of living are not good ... [but they are tolerable because they don't have to be better than they are] ... <u>it does not follow that they will always be that way and I can be happy again.</u>'

Magnification

Here, when something bad happens, you exaggerate its negativity.

'I made a faux pas when introducing my new colleague ... [which I absolutely should not have done and it's awful that I did so] ... <u>and this will have a very negative effect on my career.</u>'

Keeping things in realistic perspective

Here, when something bad happens, you view it in its proper perspective.

'I made a faux pas when introducing my new colleague ... [which I wish I had not made, but do not have to be exempt from making. It's bad that I did so, but hardly the end of the world] ... <u>and while people may remember it for a day or two, I doubt that it will have much lasting impact on my career.</u>'

Minimization

Here, you inappropriately shrink things until they appear tiny (your own desirable qualities or other people's imperfections).

'[I must do outstandingly well and I am completely useless when I do not do so] ... <u>When I have seemingly done reasonably well, this is the result of luck and anyone could have done this. Whereas if another person had done the same thing, I would acknowledge their achievement.</u>'

(Contd)

Descriptions of thinking errors and realistic and balanced alternatives	Illustrations[1]
Using the same balanced perspective for self and others	
Here, when you do something good and/or others do something bad, you can recognize such behaviour for what it is.	'[I want to do outstandingly well, but I do not have to do so. I am not useless when I do not do so]… When I or someone else has seemingly done reasonably well, <u>this may be the result of luck, but it may be because I or they fully deserved to do well.</u>'
Emotional reasoning	
Here, you assume that your negative emotions necessarily reflect the way things really are: 'I feel it, therefore it must be true.'	'Because I have performed so poorly … [as I absolutely should not have done] … <u>I feel like everybody will remember my poor performance and my strong feeling proves that they will</u>.'
Sound reasoning based on thinking and feeling	
	Because I have performed so poorly … [as I *wish*, but do not demand, that *I absolutely should not* have done] … <u>I think and feel that people will have different responses to my performance: some negative and nasty, some compassionate and empathic and some neutral, and this is probably the case</u>.'
Personalization	
Here, when a negative event occurs involving you which	'I am involved in a group presentation and things are not

Descriptions of thinking errors and realistic and balanced alternatives	Illustrations[1]
you may or may not be primarily responsible for, you see yourself definitely as the cause of it.	going well... [Since I am acting worse than I absolutely should act] ... and the audience is laughing, <u>I am sure they are laughing only at me.</u>'
Making a realistic attribution	
Here, when a negative event occurs involving you which you may or may not be primarily responsible for, you acknowledge that you may be the cause of it, but you don't assume that you definitely are. Rather, you view the event from the whole perspective before making an attribution of cause which is likely to be realistic.	'I am involved in a group presentation and things are not going well... [Since I am acting worse than I would like to do, but do not demand that I must do] ... and the audience is laughing, <u>I am not sure whom or what they are laughing at and, indeed, some might be laughing with us and not at us.</u>'

[1]In these illustrations, the beliefs (irrational and rational) are shown in square brackets and the thinking errors and realistic and balanced alternatives are underlined.

I suggest that you consult Table 9.2 when you come to formulate the realistic and balanced alternatives to your thinking errors. When you do so, I suggest that you make explicit the underlying rational belief as I have done in this chapter, if you have not already done so.

Insight

Rational beliefs are the foundations for subsequent realistic and balanced thinking.

The case of Harvey

In formulating the realistic and balanced alternative to his 'always and never' TC, Harvey recognized he had to formulate a relevant
(Contd)

and specific example of the thinking known as 'balanced thinking about the future'. Thus, instead of his distorted TC (i.e. *'If I am not creative at the start, I never will be creative'*), Harvey formulated the following realistic and balanced thought: *'I may not be creative at the beginning, but that does not mean that I can't be creative later.'* He already specified that this new TC stemmed from his rational belief as shown in Table 6.5.

How to respond to thinking consequences of irrational beliefs

There are basically three major ways to respond to the thinking consequences of irrational beliefs:

1 Use them to identify and respond to underlying irrational beliefs
2 Consider the evidence for and against the TCs and their realistic and balanced alternatives
3 Acknowledge the existence of the TCs but do not engage with them.

I will now consider these in greater depth.

USE THE TCs TO IDENTIFY AND RESPOND TO YOUR IRRATIONAL BELIEF, THEN DEVELOP AND REHEARSE THE RATIONAL BELIEF ALTERNATIVE

As inferences that are highly distorted and skewed to the negative are likely to be thinking consequences (TCs) of irrational beliefs, then one way of responding to them is to trace them back to the irrational belief and respond to this belief. There are a number of ways in which you can do this:

1 If you have time, do a written 'ABC' assessment of the episode in which you had the TCs (see Chapter 6). In doing so, seek to identify and respond to your irrational belief and develop the rational belief alternative. Then, rehearse this rational belief and if you have sufficient conviction in this rational belief then the TCs of your irrational belief will change and become more realistic and balanced. If not, then you may need to deliberately think in ways that are consistent with your developing rational belief. This involves you having previously formulated a realistic and balanced alternative to your highly distorted TCs of irrational beliefs.

2 If you do not have time to do a written 'ABC' of the episode, but you know what you are disturbing yourself about in the episode (i.e. you know what your 'A' is), then use your TCs to ask yourself the question: What demand am I making about this 'A' that has led to these TCs? Once you have formulated this irrational belief, respond to it and rehearse and develop your new rational belief, deliberately focusing on the consequent realistic and balanced TCs of this rational belief if needed (see point 1).

3 If you do not have time to do a written 'ABC' of the episode, and you do not know what you are disturbing yourself about in the episode (i.e. you do not know what your 'A' is), then use your TCs to ask yourself the question: What demand am I making in this situation that has led to these TCs? Then respond to this irrational belief, and rehearse and develop your new rational belief, again deliberately focusing on the consequent realistic and balanced TCs of this rational belief if you need to (see point 1 above).

CONSIDER THE EVIDENCE OF THE TCs AND THEIR REALISTIC ALTERNATIVES

Once you have identified the TCs of your irrational belief and formulated more realistic and balanced alternatives, stand back and consider each pair one at a time. Ask yourself the question: Which of these two thoughts best reflects the reality of the situation that I am in, the relevant details in my past and what may happen in the future?

I want to stress one important thing here. It is best to answer this question once you have identified and responded to your irrational belief and developed and rehearsed your alternative rational belief. In other words, you need to be in a reasonably rational frame of mind to answer the aforementioned question objectively. If you consider the question while in an irrational frame of mind, then you will easily find evidence to support your highly distorted TCs and to contradict the realistic and balanced TCs.

ACKNOWLEDGE THE EXISTENCE OF THE TCs, BUT DO NOT ENGAGE WITH THEM

Even if you use both the methods outlined above, you may still find that your highly distorted TCs come to mind. This is perfectly natural for two main reasons. First, you have probably had more experience thinking the TCs of irrational beliefs than the realistic and balanced TCs of rational beliefs. Second, emotionally charged TCs of irrational beliefs take quite a long time to fade even if you do not engage with them. If you engage with them after using the two approaches to TCs outlined above, you will more likely keep them in your mind rather than dismiss them from your mind.

You may continually engage with these TCs for a number of reasons:

1 You may wish to get rid of these thoughts and think that continually engaging with the thoughts will lead you to be thoroughly convinced that they are not realistic and that this thorough conviction will get rid of them. You are wrong on two counts. First, it is not likely that you will become thoroughly convinced that highly distorted TCs are false in a short period of time. Rather, you need to slowly increase your conviction in their falseness, bit by bit in small, time-limited chunks. Second, if you try to get rid of thoughts then you will only succeed in keeping them alive. There is a famous psychological experiment that shows that if you are asked to think of a white polar bear and then instruct yourself to dismiss this thought from your mind, then you will, in fact, keep this thought in your mind.

2 You may continually engage with highly distorted TCs because you are demanding certainty. If there is only a small chance that an unlikely, but highly negative, outcome will occur, this is not good enough for you. You need, or more accurately you believe you need, 100-per-cent certainty that this outcome will not happen and you will search in your mind for ways of achieving such certainty. This cognitive searching for certainty will result only in you keeping highly distorted TCs in your mind.

How can you acknowledge but not engage with highly distorted TCs?
I suggested at the outset of this section that once you have done some work on highly distorted TCs (i.e. by responding to the underlying irrational belief and by considering evidence for and against them), then you need to acknowledge their existence but not engage with them. This is what I mean by this:

WHAT IS MEANT BY ACKNOWLEDGEMENT OF TCs?
By acknowledgement of TCs, I mean that you notice the existence of these thoughts and recognize that they are highly distorted TCs

of irrational beliefs. You accept, but do not like, the fact that these thoughts are in your mind and that they will stay in your mind until they are not in your mind.

WHAT IS MEANT BY NON-ENGAGEMENT WITH TCs?

You can best understand non-engagement with the highly distorted TCs of irrational beliefs by first understanding what it means to engage with them. There are two forms of engagement with TCs: deliberate engagement and unwitting engagement.

▶ In *deliberate engagement* with TCs, you actively think about the thought and how to prevent it from becoming reality, for example. Thus, if your TC is 'Everyone will laugh at me if I make a mistake', engaging with this thought involves you thinking, for example, a) what you can do to prevent yourself from making a mistake and b) how to respond when people are laughing at you.

▶ In *unwitting engagement* with TCs, you are actively trying not to engage with the thought. Paradoxically, this has the effect that you are, in fact, engaging with it, but are not wishing to do so. Thus, if you decide to watch TV in order to distract yourself from your TCs, then you will fail since as we have seen above, the more you try not to think about something, the more you will tend to think about it. Indeed in unwitting engagement, you are engaged with thinking about what you can do so that you don't think about the TCs!!

Non-engagement with highly distorted TCs of irrational beliefs involves you getting on with life as you would if they were not in your mind. Thus, if you were planning to watch a TV programme, do so even though the TCs may still be in your mind. This is different from the above in that you are not trying to distract yourself from your TCs. You acknowledge the fact that they may be in your mind (see previous section), but you get on with whatever you have decided to get on with regardless of their presence (or absence). As you do so, accept, but do not like, that your enjoyment or concentration may be impaired to some degree by the presence of these thoughts.

People report that the effect of such acknowledgement and non-engagement is that the TCs are less present in their mind than when they engage with them or try to get rid of them.

Some useful analogies

Here are two useful analogies that people have found helpful when practising non-engaged acknowledgement of highly distorted TCs:

THE RADIO ANALOGY

'When I have very distorted thoughts, I know that they are coming from my irrational beliefs, so I think of them as voices that are on the radio. I can actively listen to them or not listen to them. The second involves them being there, but if I get on with stuff, I then soon forget that they are there. As soon as I am aware that they are not there though, they come back. But when this happens I just accept this and get on with stuff even though the radio is on.'

THE LIGHT BULB ANALOGY

'I explain it like this. Imagine that you stare at a lit light bulb and then close your eyes. What happens? You will still have images of the light bulb on your retina which will take a while to fade. If you accept that this is natural and go about your business, you will eventually note that the image of the light bulb has gone. However, if you keep returning to gaze at the light bulb, you will restimulate the retina with its image, thus keeping it alive longer on your retina.'

> **Insight**
>
> There are three ways of dealing with the thinking consequence of an irrational belief:
>
> 1 trace it back to the underlying irrational belief and question it
> 2 evaluate the evidence for and against the TC *and*
> 3 acknowledge the existence of the TC but do not engage with it.

The case of Harvey

Let's consider how Harvey responded to his highly distorted TC of his irrational belief.

You will recall that this TC was as follows: *'If I am not creative at the start, I never will be creative.'* You will also remember that Harvey formulated the following alternative realistic and balanced thought: *'I may not be creative at the beginning, but that does not mean that I can't be creative later.'*

Since Harvey had already responded to his irrational belief and was keeping his rational belief in mind, he was able to stand back and consider the evidence for and against his highly distorted TC and its realistic and balanced alternative. When he did so, he could easily see that creativity was not something lost for ever if it was not present from the start and could remember many times when he became creative having first started a task in a non-creative manner.

Having somewhat, but not totally, convinced himself of the above, Harvey began the task even though he was still aware at the back of his mind that he had the highly distorted TC. He accepted that it was there, but neither responded to it, nor tried to get rid of it. As a result, he was able to get into his work and felt the creative juices flowing before long!

You are now ready to go back and take another look at the adversity at 'A' which I previously encouraged you to assume was true and to proceed accordingly. This will be the focus of the next chapter.

THINGS TO REMEMBER

▶ The thinking consequences of irrational beliefs are highly distorted and skewed to the negative.

▶ Inferences at 'C' are more distorted than the inferences at 'A' since they have been processed by irrational beliefs while the latter have not.

▶ Common thinking errors stem from irrational beliefs.

▶ Realistic and balanced thinking alternatives to these thinking errors stem from rational beliefs.

▶ There are three ways of responding constructively to the thinking consequences of irrational beliefs:
   ▷ Use them to identify and respond to underlying irrational beliefs.
   ▷ Consider the evidence for and against the thinking consequences and their realistic and balanced alternatives.
   ▷ Acknowledge the existence of these thoughts, but do not engage with them.

10

Coming back to 'A'

In this chapter you will learn:
* *how to question the validity of 'A' which you previously assumed was true.*

As stated in Chapter 6, it is important to assume for the time being that the main inference that you made at 'A' in the specific example of your target problem is correct. Doing so will enable you to concentrate on the irrational beliefs underlying your emotional problem. Dealing effectively with 'B' helps you to be in the right frame of mind to stand back and review the main inference that you made at 'A' and to begin to plan to change problematic elements of the situation you found yourself in, if relevant.

Furthermore, if you re-examined your 'A' earlier in the emotional event that you are considering, it may occur to you that your interpretation or inference of the situation you were in was distorted and you will thus be tempted to change it. If you do change it, you might feel better as a consequence, but you would not have acquired any practice at identifying, challenging and changing your irrational beliefs. Therefore these beliefs would remain intact and be triggered the next time you encountered a similar 'A'.

Also, as your disturbed feelings originate largely from your irrational belief about 'A' rather than from 'A' itself, your attempts to reconsider this 'A', while holding an irrational belief about it, will be affected by this belief and any reconsideration of the distorted inference you may have made at 'A' will probably be short-lived. As already pointed out, having progressed in changing your irrational belief about 'A', you are likely to be in a more objective frame of mind and it is this that best facilitates accurate re-examination of 'A'.

How to re-examine 'A'

How therefore do you go about reconsidering 'A'? You will need to return to it and ask yourself whether or not this was the most realistic way of regarding the situation. This does not imply that you can know for sure that your 'A' was true or false, for there is rarely any single correct, absolute and agreed way of viewing an event. What it does mean, however, is that you can assess all the evidence available to you about the situation and formulate what may well be the 'best bet' about what has occurred.

In the next two sections I suggest various ways to examine 'A' to determine whether or not it was the most realistic way of viewing what happened in the situation in which you disturbed yourself. At the same time you can find out what Harvey did when he came to re-examine his 'A', which if you recall was: 'What I do will not be creative.'

CONSIDERING ALL RELEVANT POSSIBILITIES AND CHOOSING THE MOST LIKELY ONE

Look again at your 'ABC' and consider what you wrote under the heading 'Situation'. Then consider whether what you listed under 'A' was the most realistic approach to the situation, taking into account all the evidence at your command. This involves reviewing the inference that you made that forms 'A', considering other inferences, weighing up the possibilities and finally making a choice on the most realistic inference.

The case of Harvey

Harvey considered the likelihood that he would not be creative if he were to sit down and begin to work at his dissertation. In formulating an answer, Harvey took the following into account:

Have I been creative before when I have worked at this or other similar projects?

CASE STUDY

Answer: Yes, but not instantly. It usually takes me a while to warm to the task and the initial work may not be that creative, but once I get into my stride the creative juices begin to flow.

Have there been times when I haven't managed to be creative in a work session?

Answer: Yes, there have been occasions when I haven't been able to think of anything that creative even though I have persisted at the task.

Have there been similar tasks where I had not, at the end of the day, managed to do work that was creative?

Answer: None that I can think of. I can usually manage to inject some creativity into what I do, but there is always the first time.

Harvey then identified all the possible inferences relevant to his situation:

▶ *What I do will be creative immediately.*
▶ *What I do will not be creative immediately, but I will do creative work later in this work session.*
▶ *What I do will not be creative either immediately or later in the work session.*
▶ *What I do will never be creative.*

Finally, Harvey reviewed the evidence concerning the likelihood of these possible inferences. In doing so, he took into account what has happened in the past when he has worked on tasks similar in nature to his dissertation.

After he answered his own questions and reviewed all the relevant evidence, Harvey concluded, based on the evidence at hand, that the most likely scenario was that he would be creative later in a work session if he stayed with the task, but that it would be unlikely that his work would be creative from the outset.

....
Insight
> The goal of re-examining 'A' is not to determine the truth concerning what happened, but to accept the 'best bet' about what happened.
....

OTHER WAYS OF RE-EXAMINING 'A'

Here are some alternative ways to re-examine 'A'. You can ask yourself:

▶ 'How likely is it that "A" happened (or might happen)?'
▶ 'Would an objective jury agree that "A" happened or might happen? If not, what would the jury's verdict be?'
▶ 'Did I view (am I viewing) the situation realistically? If not, how could I have viewed (can I view) it more realistically?'
▶ 'If I asked someone whom I could trust to give me an objective opinion about the truth or falsity of my inference about the situation at hand, what would the person say to me and why? How would this person encourage me to view the situation instead?'
▶ 'If a friend had told me that she had faced (was facing or was about to face) the same situation as I faced and had made the same inference, what would I say to her about the validity of her inference and why? How would I encourage the person to view the situation instead?'

If, having repeatedly used such methods to reconsider 'A', it appears that you continue to make the same distorted inferences at 'A', then it is likely that you are doing so because you hold a relevant core irrational belief which accounts for your making these distorted inferences. I will examine the issue of core irrational beliefs in Chapter 11.

I have now covered the nuts and bolts of addressing your target problem. I will now consider how you can use these and other related skills across the board.

THINGS TO REMEMBER

▶ Remember why you put off questioning 'A' until now. You did so because earlier in the process assuming temporarily that 'A' was true helped you to identify your irrational beliefs at 'B'.

▶ The best time to come back to 'A' is when you are in a rational frame of mind about the episode in question, which you should be by this point of the REBT process.

▶ What unites different ways of re-examining 'A' is an objective consideration of the available evidence in the context of the inference you originally made at 'A' and other possible inferences you could have made.

▶ You can often not determine the truth about 'A'. You can only accept the 'best bet' about what happened given the available evidence.

11

Using established and new skills across the board

In this chapter you will learn:
- *to identify recurring themes in the specific examples you have worked on*
- *to identify core irrational beliefs and their healthy core rational belief alternatives*
- *to identify and deal with recurring highly distorted inferences at 'C'*
- *to understand how core irrational beliefs interact with uncertainty to bias the inferences that you make at 'A' and how to correct this bias.*

So far in this book you have learned the following skills:

▶ identifying and formulating your emotional problems
▶ setting and formulating realistic goals with respect to these problems
▶ choosing one problem to work on at a time and selecting a specific example of that targeted problem
▶ using the 'Situational ABC' framework to assess the chosen example and setting appropriate goals with respect to that selected example
▶ questioning your irrational beliefs and your alternative rational beliefs
▶ strengthening your conviction in your rational beliefs
▶ responding to distorted inferences at 'A' and highly distorted inferences at 'C'.

However, there is much more to REBT than helping you to deal with specific examples of your emotional problems. In this chapter, then,

I will show you how to apply these and other related skills more widely. In doing so, I will refer to the case of Melanie who had a problem with hurt.

Identifying recurring themes at 'A'

Once you have worked through a number of specific examples of your emotional problems, you may realize that you tend to disturb yourself about similar things. Put differently there may be recurring themes at 'A' in the 'ABC' framework. There are two ways of identifying such themes.

USE YOUR EMOTION

If your problems are reflected by a given problematic emotion, then this emotion has one theme or a small number of themes associated with it. I have presented the eight unhealthy negative emotions and the major themes associated with them in Table 3.1.

Using emotions to identify themes will only provide you with general themes and not necessarily their specific content. For this you need to consult the 'As' of your 'Situational ABC' forms as discussed below.

The case of Melanie

As already discussed, Melanie's major problematic emotion was hurt. As Table 3.1 shows the theme associated with hurt is 'Being unfairly treated by those close to you'. This is vague and Melanie needs to consult the specific inferences at 'A' in her specific examples of her emotional problem.

CONSULT THE 'As' IN YOUR 'SITUATIONAL ABCs'

Look at the 'ABCs' you have done on specific examples of your problems and see if you can discover any recurring themes at 'A'.

The case of Melanie

When Melanie went over her specific 'Situational ABC' forms, she discovered two major themes at 'A': 'Being let down by friends' and 'Being treated cruelly by my siblings'. Both of these themes show not just how Melanie thinks she has been treated unfairly by significant others, but how they have done so from her standpoint.

Identifying core irrational beliefs and core rational beliefs

In this section, I will consider core irrational beliefs and their core rational belief alternatives.

CORE IRRATIONAL BELIEFS

A core irrational belief is a general irrational belief that you hold about a recurring theme and which explains why you are disturbed in many situations where that theme is present or where you think that it is present.

Like a specific irrational belief, a core irrational belief comprises: a rigid belief and one major extreme belief (i.e. an awfulizing belief, a discomfort intolerance belief or a depreciation belief).

Here are some useful guidelines concerning the nature of core irrational beliefs and types of emotional problems:

1 Core irrational beliefs in self-esteem problems (including shame and guilt) involve a rigid belief and a self-depreciation belief (e.g. 'When I am involved in a situation, I must make sure that nobody gets hurt and if I don't then I am a bad person').
2 Core irrational beliefs in many forms of unhealthy anger involve a rigid belief and an other-depreciation belief (e.g. 'Other people must not try to take advantage of me and if they do that are evil').
3 Core irrational beliefs in non-ego anxiety that features highly exaggerated thinking consequences involve a rigid demand and an awfulizing belief (e.g. 'I must be in control of myself and it will be awful if I begin to lose such control').
4 Core irrational beliefs in self-discipline problems involve a rigid demand and a discomfort intolerance belief (e.g. 'Before I get down to any work I must feel like doing it and I can't bear the discomfort of doing things when I don't feel like doing so').

CORE RATIONAL BELIEFS

A core rational belief is a general rational belief that you hold about a recurring theme and which explains your constructive response in the many situations where that theme is present or where you think that it is present.

Like a specific rational belief, a core rational belief comprises: a flexible belief and one major non-extreme belief (i.e. a non-awfulizing belief, a discomfort tolerance belief or an acceptance belief).

Here are some useful guidelines concerning the nature of core rational beliefs and types of healthy responses to adversities:

1 Core rational beliefs in healthy responses to self-esteem problems involve a flexible belief and a self-acceptance belief (e.g. 'When I am involved in a situation, I want to make sure that nobody gets hurt, but sadly I don't have to do so. If I don't then I am not a bad person; I am a fallible human being with responsibility over my own behaviour in such situations, but with no responsibility over how other people act').

2 Core rational beliefs in healthy responses to anger-related themes involve a flexible belief and an other-acceptance belief (e.g. 'I don't want other people to try to take advantage of me, but that does not mean that they must not try. If they do, they are fallible and are acting badly and not evil').

3 Core rational beliefs in healthy responses to non-ego anxiety that features highly exaggerated cognitive consequences involve a flexible belief and a non-awfulizing belief (e.g. 'I want to be in control of myself, but I don't have to be in such control. It will be bad if I begin to lose such control, but it would not be awful').

4 Core rational beliefs in healthy responses to self-discipline problems involve a flexible belief and a discomfort tolerance belief (e.g. 'Before I get down to any work I prefer to feel like doing it, but I don't have to have this feeling. If I don't, it is difficult to bear, but I can bear it').

The case of Melanie

In formulating her core irrational belief and its core rational alternative Melanie did the following:

1 She took her two themes and combined them into one: 'Being treated unfairly by significant others'

(Contd)

2 She then added her rigid belief and selected the main extreme belief that was most relevant to her recurring feelings of hurt: 'I must be treated fairly by my significant others and I can't stand it when they don't.'

3 She then formulated the healthy core rational belief alternative as follows:
   'I very much want to be treated fairly by my significant others, but unfortunately this does not have to happen. I find it difficult putting up with unfairness from those close to me, but I can bear it and it is worth it to me to do so.'

Questioning core beliefs

Questioning core irrational beliefs and core rational beliefs involves similar skills to questioning specific beliefs. I suggest that you consult Chapter 7 for a detailed consideration of how to question your beliefs. The main difference between questioning specific beliefs and core beliefs is that when you do the latter you are not constrained by specific situations. This is demonstrated in the case of Melanie below. When you come to question your beliefs, while it is important to use questions concerning the truth, logic and pragmatic value of both irrational and rational beliefs, it is perhaps more important for you to use arguments that you find particularly persuasive. This is what Melanie did.

Insight
While you can apply the skills and arguments you learned when questioning your specific beliefs to the questioning of your core beliefs, you are less constrained when you question the latter and you should now have the experience and the confidence to use the arguments you find particularly persuasive.

The case of Melanie

Melanie wrote her core irrational belief and alternative core rational belief side by side on a piece of paper so that she could keep both in mind during the questioning process. Here is what she wrote:

'It would be very nice if my significant others would all treat me fairly because this is what I deserve, but sadly this is not always the case. If it had to be the case, then they would lose free will in that their behaviour would have to be guided by what I deserve rather than by what is in their mind at the time. It is a bitter pill to

swallow but, just because I don't deserve to be treated unfairly, it doesn't follow that this must not happen to me. However, since I value being treated fairly by significant others, when I think that they are treating me unfairly, I can assert myself and engage them in a dialogue about what has happened. I can do that only if I hold my core rational belief which spells out what I value, but also acknowledges that I don't have to get what I value.

'If I believe that I can't bear being treated unfairly, I would collapse and not recover, which is a ludicrous notion. What is the case is that I find being treated unfairly difficult to put up with, but I definitely can do so and it is in my interests to do so; otherwise I would not assert myself when I am treated unfairly and I would not be able to experience enjoyment in other areas of my life.'

Strengthening core rational beliefs

In Chapter 8 I discussed several ways of strengthening conviction in your specific rational beliefs. The methods I discussed included REI (rational-emotive imagery), the attack–response technique, and acting and thinking in ways that are consistent with your developing specific beliefs. In this section I will review the latter two techniques, as REI can be used only to change beliefs in specific situations.

THE ATTACK–RESPONSE TECHNIQUE

As I explained in Chapter 8, the attack–response technique is based on the idea that you can increase your conviction in your developing rational beliefs by attacking it and responding to these attacks until you can make no more attacks. Unlike REI, you can use this technique to increase your conviction in your core rational beliefs. In doing so, you should be able to apply this learning to a broad range of situations defined by the theme of the belief. As with using this technique with specific rational beliefs, you begin by stating the core rational belief and rating your degree of conviction in it; you also re-rate it at the end to ascertain the extent of conviction change.

The case of Melanie

What follows is an excerpt from Melanie's use of the attack–response technique in attempting to increase her conviction in her core rational belief.

(Contd)

ACTING AND THINKING IN WAYS THAT ARE CONSISTENT WITH ONE'S CORE RATIONAL BELIEFS

In my view, the most potent way of changing your core irrational beliefs (CIBs) and increasing your conviction in your core rational beliefs (CRBs) is to act and think in ways that are inconsistent with the former and consistent with the latter in specific situations defined by the theme of the core beliefs.

In some cases where these situations readily occur then you have plenty of opportunities to develop your core rational beliefs. In other cases, you will have to actively seek out such situations. In both cases, you need to rehearse specific variants of your CRB while acting and thinking in ways that are consistent with this belief.

The case of Perry

Thus, Perry was generally scared of talking to strangers because he held the core irrational belief: *'I must not sound common to strangers and, if I do, I am unlikeable.'* This led him to either remain silent when he was with strangers or to affect a posh voice when he spoke to them. Also, his subsequent thinking was characterized by overestimates of strangers noticing his 'common' accent and thinking negatively of him for so doing.

In working to strengthen his core rational belief, Perry took every opportunity to speak to strangers in his natural voice, while rehearsing a specific variant of his CRB (i.e. *'I would prefer not to sound common to strangers, but I am not exempt from doing so and neither do I have to be so exempt. If I sound common, I am not unlikeable. Rather I am a person capable of being liked and disliked'*). As Perry did so, he reminded himself that, in speaking up, he would get a variety of different responses to his natural accent. However, he refrained from using this thinking as a reassurance strategy.

It is important not to be perfectionist about your behaviour and thinking on this point. The important thing is that the ratio between CRB-strengthening behaviour and CIB-strengthening behaviour is in favour of the former. The higher the ratio the more likely it is that you will strengthen your conviction in your core rational belief. The same is also the case with subsequent thinking. The more such thinking is realistic and balanced, the more likely it is that you will strengthen your CRB.

....

Insight
Strengthening your conviction in a core rational belief involves you rehearsing specific variants of this core belief in relevant situations defined by your

(Contd)

theme at 'A'. It is most important that you keep your behaviour and thinking consistent with both the specific rational belief and the more general core rational belief.

The case of Melanie

If you recall, Melanie's core rational belief was as follows:

> 'I very much want to be treated fairly by my significant others, but unfortunately this does not have to happen. I find it difficult putting up with unfairness from those close to me, but I can bear it and it is worth it to me to do so.'

In order to strengthen her conviction in this CRB, Melanie rehearsed specific variants of this belief as she did the following:

▶ She approached people close to her whom she thought were likely to treat her in an uncaring manner and asserted herself about being treated unfairly while rehearsing the relevant specific variant of her CRB.
▶ She reminded herself that, while some people close to her at some points did treat her unfairly, others treated her fairly. However, she did not overuse this as a self-reassurance seeking strategy, but as a way of putting things into perspective.

Melanie was able to keep the ratio of her constructive behaviour to unconstructive behaviour at 4:1 and of her balanced and realistic thinking to skewed and unrealistic thinking to 3:1.

Melanie persisted in seeking out situations in which it was likely that she would be treated unfairly and the more she kept her behaviour and thinking in line with her developing CRB, the greater her conviction in it became, and this then had a positive impact on her constructive behaviour and balanced and realistic thinking.

Identifying and responding to recurring highly distorted inferences at 'C'

You will recall that in the 'Situational ABC' model of psychological disturbance and health that I have used in this book, 'C' stands for the thinking consequences of irrational or rational beliefs. I have argued that the thinking consequences of specific irrational beliefs tend to be highly distorted and unrealistic and this is also the case when we consider the thinking consequences of core irrational beliefs.

There are a number of ways to deal with recurring highly distorted inferences at 'C' and in what follows I will consider them (see also Chapter 9).

IDENTIFY THE RECURRING HIGHLY DISTORTED INFERENCES

In Chapter 9 I discussed what constitutes a highly distorted inference. To recap, an inference is a thought that goes beyond the data at hand. It may be accurate or inaccurate. A highly distorted inference is a thought that goes well beyond the data at hand and involves you thinking in very exaggerated and negative ways. As such, highly distorted inferences are very likely to be inaccurate. Thus, if you believe that you must not make a mistake in public and that if you do 'everybody will criticize me', then this latter thought is highly distorted in that it predicts that all the people present will respond in a negative way. This is unlikely to be true unless your mistake is so bad to occasion such a response from everybody present.

So far, I have discussed highly distorted thoughts at 'C'. However, you may also think in pictures and these images may also be highly distorted in nature. Thus, rather than have the verbally based thought 'everybody will criticize me', you may have an image where you see in your mind's eye everybody present criticizing you for the mistake that you made.

If you notice that you routinely have such highly distorted thoughts or images, then there are a number of ways of dealing with them which I will now discuss.

GO BACK TO YOUR CORE IRRATIONAL BELIEF (CIB) AND QUESTION IT

The existence of recurring highly distorted thoughts and images at 'C' indicates that your core irrational belief is active and needs to be questioned. Thus, you can use the presence of these highly distorted cognitions to go back to 'B' and briefly question your CIB and ensure that your core rational belief (CRB) is in place.

When you return to 'B' at this point, please note that your goal is not to completely convince yourself of the rationality of your CRB and of the irrationality of your CIB, but to take a step towards this outcome. Think of conviction as being on a 0–100-per-cent continuum (as used in the attack–response technique described in Chapter 8 and earlier in this chapter).

IDENTIFY THE THINKING ERROR(S) IN YOUR RECURRING HIGHLY DISTORTED INFERENCES

In Chapter 9 I discussed the major errors that you make when your inferences at 'C' are highly distorted. These are known as thinking errors and, if you need to, I suggest that you review this material at this point. It is useful for you to note the thinking error and appreciate what it is about your subsequent thinking that is distorted.

DEVELOP REALISTIC AND BALANCED ALTERNATIVES TO YOUR RECURRING HIGHLY DISTORTED INFERENCES

It is important that you develop realistic and balanced alternatives to your recurring highly distorted inferences. If you do not do so, then you will tend to continue to think in such highly distorted ways, given that you have no alternative thoughts to think.

WHEN TO RESPOND TO YOUR RECURRING HIGHLY DISTORTED INFERENCES AND ENGAGE WITH REALISTIC AND BALANCED THINKING

Much of CBT is based on the principle that when you identify your distorted thinking it is important that you examine and respond to it and think healthily instead. Thus, when you identify your recurring highly distorted thinking that stems from your core irrational beliefs, it is important that you respond to it and engage with the realistic and balanced alternatives. However, there are exceptions to this principle which I will detail below.

WHEN NOT TO RESPOND TO YOUR RECURRING HIGHLY DISTORTED INFERENCES NOR ENGAGE WITH REALISTIC AND BALANCED THINKING

When you have done some work at questioning your core beliefs and have responded to your recurring highly distorted inferences that stem from your core irrational beliefs, you may well find that you still have these highly distorted thoughts in your mind even though you are developing your core rational beliefs.

I liken this phenomenon to staring at a light bulb and then closing your eyes. When you do this you will still see the light as an after image on your retina. The best way to deal with this is to accept it and don't go back to look at the light.

In the same way, when your highly distorted thoughts remain in your mind despite your efforts to respond to them and to the core irrational beliefs that underpin them, then these are what I call 'cognitive reverberations' – thoughts that are equivalent to the reverberating image of the light on your retina. The best way to deal with such thoughts is to acknowledge their existence, understand that they are reverberating thoughts and don't engage with them. Rather, pursue your goals while such thoughts stay in your mind. If you allow yourself to do this then these thoughts will go far more quickly than if you re-engage with them, distract yourself from them or attempt to suppress them.

The case of Melanie

This is how Melanie dealt with her recurring highly distorted inferences:

1 She first identified her recurring highly distorted inferences:
   'I am always being taken advantage of. I can't trust anyone to treat me well.'
2 When Melanie first identified these highly distorted thoughts, she used them to go back to her core irrational belief (CIB) *'I must be treated fairly by my significant others and I can't stand it when they don't'* and to question it (see the section on questioning core beliefs).
3 Melanie then identified the following thinking errors in her recurring highly distorted thinking:
   ▷ always-and-never thinking: *'I am always being taken advantage of'*
   ▷ all-or-none thinking: *'I can't trust anyone to treat me well.'*

   Referring to these errors by name helped Melanie to distance herself from this way of thinking.
4 Melanie developed the following realistic and balanced alternatives to her recurring highly distorted inferences:
   'I am sometimes taken advantage of, but this does not always happen. I can trust some people to treat me well, but not everyone.'
   (Contd)

5 Whenever Melanie first identified her recurring highly distorted inferences she responded to them and engaged in thinking the realistic and balanced thoughts. However, she did so mindful of the fact that her goal was to increase her conviction in these latter thoughts and not to achieve total conviction in them.

6 After Melanie had responded to her recurring highly distorted thinking, she recognized that these thoughts would reverberate in her mind for a while. As such she did not re-engage with them, but accepted their continued existence and let them be as she got on with whatever she needed to do at the time. Although Melanie felt tempted to re-engage with her highly distorted thinking, she refrained from doing so.

Insight

Respond to your highly distorted thinking in small doses. When these thoughts continue to reverberate in your mind, let them do so without engaging with them and do whatever it is you would have done if they were absent.

Why you make distorted inferences at 'As'

As you will recall, when you are working on a specific example of your problem using the 'ABC' framework, it is important that you begin by assuming temporarily that your adversity at 'A' is correct, even though it may seem distorted. Doing so will help you to identify your irrational beliefs at 'B' which, according to REBT, are at the root of your emotional problems. If you corrected the distortion at 'A' at the outset, then you would not be motivated to identify, question and change your irrational beliefs at 'B'. As such, you would be vulnerable to disturbance as your irrational beliefs would remain unchallenged.

As I discussed in Chapter 10, the time to question your 'A', if it seems distorted, is after you have questioned your beliefs at 'B' and are committed to strengthening your rational beliefs. Once you have done this, the following question remains: Why do you make distorted inferences at 'A'?

Here is how REBT explains this process. We have seen that, when you disturb yourself across a range of similar situations, it is because you hold a core irrational belief. Now you tend to bring your core beliefs to situations which are related to themes about which you disturb yourself. Thus, if your core irrational belief is 'I must not be criticized by authority figures', then you will tend to bring this belief to situations where there is a possibility of you being criticized by authority figures.

To this scenario, let's add the concept of uncertainty, in particular not knowing that the adversity at 'A' will not happen. When you add this type of uncertainty to your core irrational belief (e.g. 'I must not be criticized by authority figures'), then this core belief is modified to incorporate uncertainty (i.e. 'I must know that the authority figures will not criticize me'). When you bring this core belief to situations where there is uncertainty about whether or not you will be criticized by authority figures, then, unless you can convince yourself that these figures will not criticize you, you will tend to think that they *will* criticize you. When you do that, you have created a distorted inference at 'A'. This is shown in Figure 11.1.

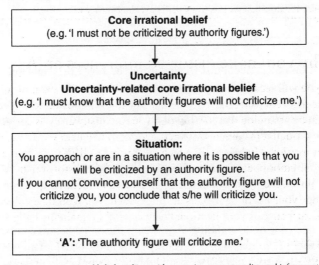

Figure 11.1 How a core irrational belief combines with uncertainty to create a distorted inference at 'A'.

You can use this information to correct any biases you have when you make inferences at 'A'. However, remember to continue to identify and respond to your irrational beliefs at 'B'.

In Chapter 13 I will discuss how you can maintain and enhance the gains that you have made so far. But first I will consider how you can deal with lapses and prevent relapse.

THINGS TO REMEMBER

▶ When you disturb yourself across the board then use your recurring unhealthy negative emotions and the specific 'As' you have assessed in your 'Situational ABC' forms to identify recurring themes at 'A'.

▶ It is likely you hold core irrational beliefs about these general themes.

▶ Develop core rational beliefs and question both using your established questioning skills but focus on arguments you find particularly persuasive.

▶ Strengthen your core rational beliefs using a more general version of the attack–response technique and extend the principle of rehearsing your rational belief while acting and thinking in ways consistent with this belief in situations where your general themes are present in specific form.

▶ Don't be perfectionist when putting the above principle into practice. As long as the ratio of constructive behaviour to unconstructive behaviour and of balanced and realistic thinking to skewed and distorted thinking is weighted towards the first terms, then change will occur.

▶ Respond to your highly distorted thinking in small doses and then let them be in your mind as you go on with the business of life.

▶ Use your understanding of how core irrational beliefs combine with the principle of uncertainty to form distorted inferences at 'A' to correct any biases you find in your thinking, but do not neglect the central task of belief change.

12

Dealing with lapses and preventing relapse

In this chapter you will learn:
- *how to distinguish between a lapse and a relapse*
- *about the relapse prevention sequence and how to use it.*

Once you have made progress in overcoming your problems and
you have used your REBT skills across the board, you need to deal
with lapses to continued progress and thus help yourself to prevent
relapse. A lapse is a temporary and non-serious return to a problem
state while a relapse is a more enduring, serious return to that state.
In order to help yourself to prevent a relapse you need to use a
sequence of steps to do so.

The relapse prevention sequence and how to use it

In using the relapse prevention sequence which I will discuss below,
please bear in mind that this sequence and the order in which it is
presented are suggestions and you should not follow them slavishly.
Use the sequence as a guide and modify it according to your own
situation.

REVIEW WHAT YOU HAVE ACHIEVED SO FAR AND THINK THROUGH HOW YOU CAN APPLY WHAT YOU HAVE LEARNED TO FUTURE RELATED PROBLEMS

This initial step in the relapse prevention sequence is related to and
builds on the work that you did in the previous chapter. In order to
know how to deal with relapse you need to know what you have

achieved so far in the REBT process of self-help. It is helpful to go back to your goals and ask yourself to what extent you have achieved them and what you have learned that has enabled you to have made the progress that you have made. Using this knowledge you can begin to think through how you can apply this learning to related problems that you may encounter in the future.

DEVELOP RATIONAL BELIEFS ABOUT LAPSES

I have defined a lapse as a temporary and non-serious return to a problem state. As such, it is very likely that you will experience a number of lapses along the path to personal change. Despite this, it is important that you develop rational beliefs about experiencing such lapses. Doing so will help you to learn from these lapses. On the other hand, if you hold a set of irrational beliefs about lapsing, then you will disturb yourself about doing so which will both impede you from learning from these lapses and thus increase the chances of experiencing a relapse, which I have defined as a more enduring, serious return to a problem state. What follows is a set of rational beliefs that you can adapt for your own use in thinking about and responding to the inevitable lapses along the way to personal change:

▶ I would prefer not to experience lapses, but I am not immune from them and nor do I have to be.
▶ It is unfortunate to experience lapses, but not the end of the world.
▶ It is a struggle to put up with lapsing, but I can tolerate it and it is worth it to me to do so.
▶ I am a fallible human being who experiences lapses along the way to personal change. I am not less of a person for doing so.
▶ The world is not a rotten place for allowing lapses to occur. It is a complex mixture of the good, the bad and the neutral.

If you develop such a rational philosophy then you will be best placed to deal with the main reason why people relapse – failure to deal with factors that render them particularly vulnerable to lapsing.

> **Insight**
> Developing rational beliefs about lapses will help you to deal with them effectively. If you hold irrational beliefs about such lapses, you will avoid thinking about them and thus will not make plans about how to respond to them.

IDENTIFY FACTORS TO WHICH YOU REMAIN VULNERABLE

As I have just said, vulnerability factors are factors that if you encounter them render you vulnerable to experiencing your problems once again. A vulnerability factor may be external to you or internal. Typical external vulnerability factors are negative situations involving other people which you find particularly problematic and which are either inherently bound up with your main problems or which have a bearing on them. Thus, if you are trying to give up smoking, being with other people who smoke and who urge you to join them may serve as an external vulnerability factor to you.

Typical internal vulnerability factors include urges, thoughts and a sense of discomfort. For example, if you are working towards greater self-discipline and you experience an urge to do something that will take you away from self-disciplined behaviour, then this constitutes an internal vulnerability factor.

A vulnerability factor may be the same as the 'A' that you originally identified when you were first working on your problems or it may be different, albeit related. The most reliable way of identifying a vulnerability factor is to consider times when you lapsed back into your problem having made progress. If such lapses occurred in situations that were similar, then a vulnerability factor is likely to be present in such situations.

Freda had made considerable progress in dealing with her unhealthy anger. However, in the course of a week she lost her temper twice with her son when he interrupted her when she was watching her favourite TV programme. In such circumstances it is best to use the 'Situational ABC' framework that I discussed earlier in this book (see Chapter 6) in order to pinpoint the vulnerability factor. Table 12.1 shows how to apply this framework in general terms to the identification of a vulnerability factor and Table 12.2 shows how Freda used it in her case. As it turned out, Freda's vulnerability factor was somewhat different to the 'As' to which she originally responded with unhealthy anger. Her original 'As' were people getting away with inconsiderate behaviour and her vulnerability factor was her son deliberately provoking her.

Table 12.1 The application of the 'Situational ABC'
framework to the identification of a vulnerability
factor.

'Situation'	=	The situation in which the lapse occurred
'A'	=	Vulnerability factor (The aspect of the situation to which you had the unhealthy response)
'B'	=	Irrational beliefs
'C'	=	Unhealthy response

Table 12.2 How Freda applied the 'Situational ABC'
framework to the identification of her vulnerability
factor.

'Situation'	=	*My son interrupted me when I was watching my favourite TV programme*
'A'	=	Vulnerability factor = *He knows that I am working on my unhealthy anger and he is deliberately provoking me*
'B'	=	*My son must not deliberately provoke me; he is evil for doing so*
'C'	=	*Unhealthy anger*

DETERMINE HOW YOU WOULD DEAL CONSTRUCTIVELY WITH THESE VULNERABILITY FACTORS SHOULD YOU ENCOUNTER THEM

Once you have used the 'Situational ABC' framework to identify your vulnerability factor at 'A', then you can continue to use it to identify and respond to the irrational beliefs at 'B' in dealing with specific examples where you did not deal with your vulnerability factors in constructive ways. You do this in the same way as you did when working on specific examples of your problem (see Chapter 6).

Using the 'Situational ABC' model

The following steps should serve as a reminder concerning how to use the 'Situational ABC' framework:

1 Specify your unhealthy responses at 'C'. These will be i) an unhealthy negative emotion; ii) an unconstructive behaviour or

action tendency and, if relevant, iii) a highly distorted thought or thoughts, skewed to the negative.

2 Identify the irrational beliefs at 'B' that underpin the above responses. Specify the rigid belief and the one extreme belief that best explains your unconstructive responses. Here you should select either an awfulizing belief, a discomfort intolerance belief or a depreciation belief (self-, other- or life-).

3 Specify the healthy responses at 'C' that you are aiming for when meeting your vulnerability factor at 'A'. Given that the vulnerability factor is a negative event, your emotional goal will be negative, but healthy, your behavioural goal will be constructive and your thinking goal will be realistic.

4 Identify the rational beliefs at 'B' that underpin your emotional, behavioural and thinking goals. Specify the flexible belief and the one non-extreme belief that best explains your healthy responses. Here you should select either a non-awfulizing belief, a discomfort tolerance belief or an acceptance belief (self-, other- or life-).

5 Question your rational and irrational beliefs until you can see that the former are true, logical and helpful and that the latter are false, illogical and unhelpful.

6 Commit yourself to strengthening your rational beliefs.

Using imagery rehearsal of rational beliefs
Once you have committed yourself to strengthening the rational beliefs that underpin how you would like to respond emotionally to your vulnerability factor, you need to use some of the strengthening techniques that I discussed in Chapter 8. In particular, you can use rational-emotive imagery as follows:

1 Close your eyes and see yourself facing your vulnerability factor and make yourself feel emotionally disturbed as you do so.

2 While you are still facing the vulnerability factor change your emotional response to the way you would like to feel in relation to the factor (this will be a healthy negative emotion, or HNE) and hold that response for a few minutes.

3 Ensure that you changed your emotional response by changing your irrational beliefs to their rational belief equivalents. If not, repeat the technique until you have done so.

Repeat this exercise three times a day until your emotional response to the vulnerability factor is healthy and negative.

Using imagery rehearsal of constructive behaviour

You can also use imagery to rehearse seeing yourself act in constructive ways when facing your vulnerability factor. Some people find this a very useful step to take before taking action in the face of their actual vulnerability factor, while for others this step is not necessary or is even counterproductive. You might like to try out this technique to determine for yourself whether or not it is likely to be helpful as preparation for taking action in the real world.

If you do decide to use imagery rehearsal to imagine yourself acting constructively in facing your vulnerability factor, then the more vividly you can imagine doing this, the better. However, some people do not have a store of vivid imagery and, if this applies to you, don't worry. You can still use imagery with benefit. Here is what you do:

Select a vulnerability factor that is challenging for you to deal with, but you do not find overwhelming.

1 Be clear with yourself what your vulnerability factor is. This is likely to be the 'A' in the 'Situational ABC' framework.
2 Be clear with yourself how you are going to deal constructively with this vulnerability factor.
3 Choose a situation in which it is likely that you will encounter your vulnerability factor.
4 Get yourself into the right frame of mind by rehearsing your relevant rational beliefs.
5 See yourself facing your vulnerability factor and dealing with it constructively. It is better to see yourself struggle than to see yourself showing unrealistic mastery.

Repeat this imagery exercise three times a day until you are ready to face the vulnerability in reality.

PUT THIS CONSTRUCTIVE PLAN INTO ACTION BY FACING YOUR VULNERABILITY FACTORS

You are now ready to face your vulnerability factor armed with your rational beliefs and a clear idea of how you are going to act when you face it. You can use the principle that I have called 'challenging, but not overwhelming' here. In deciding that facing your vulnerability factor in a given context constitutes a challenge for you, but is not overwhelming, you are not, in common parlance, 'biting off more than you can chew' by taking this step. It is useful to get yourself in the right frame of mind by rehearsing your rational belief before you take action and to hold this belief in mind while you are taking action. While the former is almost always possible, the latter is more difficult given that you may have to concentrate fully on what you are doing and may not have time to rehearse your rational belief *in situ*, even briefly. Don't worry if this is the case, since your pre-action rehearsal of your rational belief will often be enough to carry you through and, if not, you can review and learn from this experience later.

The case of Kirsty

Here is how Kirsty dealt with her vulnerability *in situ* by implementing the material that I have presented in this section. Kirsty was working to give up smoking and identified that her major vulnerability factor was going out for a drink with her colleagues after work. Several of these colleagues smoked and would often encourage Kirsty to join them outside for a *'cigarette and a natter'*, both of which she enjoyed. Up to now, Kirsty had dealt with this vulnerability factor by either avoiding altogether joining the group for drinks after work or by declining their invitation to join them outside. Kirsty came to realize that such avoidance was not a good long-term approach to dealing with her vulnerability factor and thus she decided to deal with her vulnerability factor head on.

By using the 'Situational ABC' framework, Kirsty identified that her vulnerability factor was *'being thought boring by my smoking colleagues'* and her irrational belief was *'I must not be thought boring by my work colleagues and if I am it proves that I am a boring person'*. Her goal was to go outside with her colleagues for conversation but decline offers of cigarettes. In order to do this, Kirsty recognized that she had to develop and strengthen the following rational belief:

> *'I don't want to be thought boring by my work colleagues, but that does not mean that they must not think of me in this way. If they do, it does not mean that I am a boring person. I am the same person whether they find me interesting or boring. I am a fallible complex person capable of boring and interesting people.'*

Kirsty practised rational-emotive imagery (REI – see above and Chapter 8) to strengthen this rational belief and then used

(Contd)

imagery rehearsal to see herself going outside with her friends and rehearsing this belief while declining all offers of a cigarette. She then implemented this in real life. Thus, she accepted an invitation to go outside for a *'chat and a ciggie'* with four of her female smoking friends. They put her under quite a bit of pressure to take a cigarette, but less than she expected and she was surprised by two of them saying that they wished that they could quit smoking. From then on, Kirsty took every opportunity to join her smoking friends, but only for their cigarette-related conversation. While at times Kirsty was tempted to have a cigarette, she accepted her urge to take one, but did not act on it. Rather, she rehearsed the idea that while she wanted a cigarette at that point, she did not have to have one.

Insight

Use your established REBT skills to deal with your vulnerability factor. First, prepare the ground by using the 'Situational ABC' framework and imagery techniques. Then, face your vulnerability factor while rehearsing the appropriate rational belief, but do so sensibly.

REVIEW YOUR EXPERIENCES OF DEALING WITH THESE VULNERABILITY FACTORS AND LEARN FROM SUCH REVIEWS

Once you have taken action in the face of your vulnerability factors several times, it is important that you stand back and review your experiences of doing so in order to learn from experiences. Doing so will help you to fine tune your responses to your vulnerability factors.

The case of Kirsty

Kirsty did this and realized that what was particularly helpful to her in responding to invitations to accept a cigarette was admitting to her friends that she wanted a cigarette, but because her plan was to stop smoking, she was not going to have one since she did not need one. Reminding herself of this rational belief helped her to ask her friends to keep offering her cigarettes so that she had the opportunity of declining the offer.

DEVELOP RATIONAL BELIEFS ABOUT RELAPSE

As I mentioned at the beginning of this chapter, a relapse is a more enduring, serious return to a problem, colloquially referred to as 'going back to square one'. So far in this chapter I have discussed the steps that you need to take to deal with lapses and your vulnerability factors and thus help to prevent relapse. However, as it is possible for you to relapse, it is important to face up to and deal with this possibility. Once you have done so, ask yourself what it is about relapsing that you would disturb yourself about. As you will know this represents your 'A' in the 'Situational ABC' framework. In my experience, people disturb themselves about two major 'As': weakness ('If I relapse, it reveals a weakness about me') and loss of self-control ('If I relapse, it means that I have lost self-control').

Develop rational beliefs about weakness-related relapse
When you disturb yourself about relapsing because it reveals a weakness, you tend to experience shame which motivates you to avoid dealing with the possibility of relapse. You tend to think that people will look down on you and dismiss you should you relapse.

If you experience shame about relapsing, it's important that you develop the following rational beliefs which you need to put into your own words:

▶ *Flexible belief*: 'I really don't want to be weak and relapse, but sadly and regretfully I am not immune from doing so and nor do I have to be so immune.'
▶ *Non-awfulizing belief*: 'It would be unfortunate if I were to be weak and relapse, but it would not be the end of the world.'
▶ *Discomfort tolerance belief*: 'It would be a struggle for me to put up with being weak and relapsing, but I could tolerate it and it is worth it to me to do so.'
▶ *Self-acceptance belief*: 'If I relapse, that would be bad but it would not prove that I am a weak pathetic person. It means that I am a complex, unrateable, fallible human being.'

Develop rational beliefs about relapse related to loss of self-control
When you disturb yourself about relapsing because it indicates that you have experienced a loss of self-control, you tend to experience anxiety which leads you to make a desperate attempt to regain such self-control. However, because your attempt is based on desperation, it leads you to become more anxious rather than less anxious and this increases the negativity of your subsequent thoughts about the extent and implications of such loss of self-control (i.e. your subsequent thinking is highly distorted and skewed to the negative).

If you experience anxiety about the loss of self-control that accompanies relapse, then again it's important that you develop the following rational beliefs which you need to put into your own words:

▶ *Flexible belief*: 'I really don't want to relapse and lose self-control, but sadly and regretfully I am not immune from doing so and nor do I have to be so immune.'
▶ *Non-awfulizing belief*: 'It would be unfortunate if I were to relapse and lose self-control, but it would not be the end of the world.'
▶ *Discomfort tolerance belief*: 'It would be a struggle for me to put up with relapsing and losing self-control, but I could tolerate it and it is worth it to me to do so.'
▶ *Life-acceptance belief*: 'If I relapse and lose self-control, that would be bad but it would not prove that life is all bad for allowing this to happen to me. Life is a complex mixture of the good, the bad and the neutral.'

Develop rational beliefs about relapse in general
In the above two sections, I have considered two of the most common problems that people tend to have about relapsing (i.e. being weak and losing self-control) and I have outlined the rational beliefs that you need to develop if you experience one or both of these issues. However, some people disturb themselves about the fact of relapse without any surplus meaning and, if this applies to you, it is important that you develop a set of rational beliefs about the fact of relapse. I will list these now, but suggest that you modify them to suit your own situation:

▶ *Flexible belief*: 'I really don't want to relapse, but sadly and regretfully I am not immune from relapse and nor do I have to be so immune.'
▶ *Non-awfulizing belief*: 'It would be unfortunate if I were to relapse, but it would not be the end of the world.'
▶ *Discomfort tolerance belief*: 'It would be a struggle for me to put up with relapsing, but I could tolerate it and it is worth it to me to do so.'
▶ *Self-acceptance belief*: 'If I relapse, that would be bad but it would not prove that I am a weak pathetic person. It means that I am a complex, unrateable, fallible human being.'
▶ *Life-acceptance belief*: 'If I relapse, life is not bad. It is a complex place where many good, bad and neutral things happen including relapse.'

Learn from relapse

If you develop and implement a rational philosophy about relapsing then you will calm down about the prospect of it happening. This will help you to put the likelihood of you relapsing into perspective and help you to realize that you will lessen the chance of doing so if you are diligent in learning from your relapses and if you deal adequately with your vulnerability factors.

Your rational philosophy will also help you to learn from relapse should you, in fact, actually experience one. It will help you to review times where your lapses became more serious and what you would have needed to have done to have dealt with these effectively, thus reducing the chances that you would relapse. Then, you would implement this learning, thus helping to protect you from relapsing in future.

In the next chapter I will discuss how you can maintain the gains that you have made in using REBT.

THINGS TO REMEMBER

▶ Lapses are an inevitable part of the change process.

▶ The best way to deal with lapses is to first develop rational beliefs about them.

▶ In order to prevent relapse, the first thing you need to do is to deal with and learn from your lapses.

▶ Most importantly, relapse prevention depends on you identifying and dealing effectively with your vulnerability factors.

▶ Prepare yourself to face your vulnerability factors by using the 'Situational ABC' framework and through imagery.

▶ When you face your vulnerability factors, use the 'challenging but not overwhelming' concept and rehearse relevant rational beliefs before and during the experience.

▶ As with lapses, it is best to develop rational beliefs about relapse. If you do, you are less likely to relapse than you would be if you held irrational beliefs about it.

▶ If you do relapse, don't disturb yourself about this grim reality but learn from it.

13

Maintaining your gains

In this chapter you will learn:
- *the importance of taking responsibility for maintaining the gains you have made by using REBT*
- *how best to maintain your gains*
- *a philosophy of dealing with obstacles to maintaining your gains.*

As I discussed in Chapter 12, personal change, like the course of true love, rarely runs smoothly. Thus, once you have made progress in addressing your problems, you cannot afford to rest on your laurels. You need to take responsibility for actively maintaining the gains that you have made and even enhancing them if you want to capitalize on the skills that you have learned in this book. In this chapter, then, I will focus on showing you how you can maintain the gains that you have made and the philosophy you need to develop to enable you to deal with obstacles to gain maintenance.

Take responsibility for maintaining your gains

As we have seen, one of the cornerstones of the REBT approach to personal change is that while events contribute to your responses, what you believe about these events is more important in determining your responses to these events. Thus, if you hold a set of irrational beliefs about adversities, then you will respond unconstructively to these events. By contrast, if you hold a set of rational beliefs about the same adversities, then your responses will be constructive. Therefore, REBT argues that you need to take responsibility for:

1 helping to create your disturbance (through your irrational beliefs) *and*

2   dealing with your disturbance (by questioning and changing
    your beliefs to rational beliefs and by strengthening these
    rational beliefs by acting and thinking in ways that are consistent
    with them).

It follows from this that, if you are largely responsible for whether
or not you disturb yourself about adversities at 'A', then you are also
largely responsible for maintaining the gains that you have made by
using the principles outlined in this book.

In Chapter 12 I discussed how you can deal with lapses to prevent
relapsing. In this chapter I will show you, more generally, what you
can do to maintain your gains once you have made progress.

Insight
> If you don't take responsibility for maintaining your gains, then it is unlikely
> that you will maintain them.

How to maintain your gains

More than 25 years ago, Albert Ellis, the founder of REBT,
made a number of important suggestions concerning how you can
maintain the gains that you have made from using REBT principles
and techniques (Ellis 1984). I have borrowed liberally from his ideas
in this section. Here are the suggestions:

1   When you have made gains and then begin to backslide into your
    old problems, remember as precisely as you can what thoughts,
    feelings and behaviours you once changed to bring about your
    improvement. If you again feel disturbed, think back to how you
    previously used REBT principles to make yourself undisturbed.
    For example, you may remember that:
    ▷ you accepted yourself whenever authority figures
       criticized you (or you thought that they might) rather than
       condemning yourself as worthless as you did previously
    ▷ you tolerated the discomfort of asking your neighbours
       to refrain from making a noise, when you had previously
       thought that you could not bear to do this
    ▷ you decided to spend time with your mother-in-law for the
       sake of your spouse and worked to accept her as a fallible
       human being for her interfering behaviour.

Remind yourself of the beliefs, thoughts, feelings and behaviours that you have changed and how you changed them. Use that information when you notice that you have begun to backslide.

2 Keep rehearsing rational beliefs or coping statements based on these beliefs, such as: 'It's great to be accepted, but I can fully accept myself as a person and enjoy life considerably even when I am rejected!' Don't merely repeat these statements by rote, but really think them through many times until you really begin to believe and feel that they are true. However, don't over-rehearse such statements.

3 Keep seeking for, discovering and questioning your irrational beliefs with which you are once again disturbing yourself. Take each important irrational belief – such as 'I have to succeed and I am not a worthwhile person if I don't!' – and keep asking yourself: 'Why is this belief true?', 'Where is the evidence that my worth to myself, and my enjoyment of living, utterly depend on my succeeding at something?', 'In what way would I be totally unacceptable as a human if I failed at an important task or test?' Keep questioning your irrational beliefs persistently and persuasively wherever you see that you are letting them creep back again. And even when you don't actively hold them, realize that they may arise once more; so bring them to your consciousness, and preventatively – and persuasively – dispute them.

Keep risking and doing things that you would normally avoid doing – such as asking people out on a date, job hunting or creative writing. Once you have partly overcome one of your anxieties, keep acting against it on a regular basis. If you feel uncomfortable in forcing yourself to do things that you are unrealistically afraid of doing, don't allow yourself to avoid doing them – thereby preserving your discomfort for ever! Make yourself as uncomfortable as you can be in order to address effectively your irrational fears and to become unanxious and comfortable later.

4 Try to see clearly the difference between healthy negative feelings – such as those of sadness, remorse and disappointment, when you do not get some of the important things you want – and unhealthy negative feelings – such as those of depression, unhealthy guilt and shame under the same circumstances. Realize that you are capable of changing your unhealthy negative feelings to healthy negative ones by changing your rigid and

extreme beliefs to their flexible and non-extreme counterparts.
Thus, take your depressed feelings and work on them until you
feel only sad and sorry. Take your anxious feelings and work on
them until you feel only concerned and vigilant. Use the variety
of REBT techniques that I have described in this book to do this.

5 Avoid self-defeating procrastination. Do unpleasant tasks fast –
today! If you still procrastinate, reward yourself with certain
things that you enjoy – for example, reading and socializing – only
after you have performed the tasks that you easily avoid. If this
won't work, give yourself a severe penalty – such as talking to a
person whom you find boring for two hours or giving away a £20
note to an unworthy cause! – every time that you procrastinate.

6 Show yourself that it is an absorbing challenge and something
of an adventure to maintain your emotional health and to keep
yourself reasonably happy no matter what kind of misfortunes
assail you. Make the uprooting of your misery one of the
most important things in your life – something you are utterly
determined to steadily work at achieving. Fully acknowledge
that you almost always have some choice about how to think,
feel and behave, and throw yourself actively into making that
choice for yourself.

7 Remember – and use – the three main insights of REBT:

▷ *Insight 1*: You largely choose to disturb yourself about
the unpleasant events of your life, although you may
be encouraged to do so by external happenings and by
social learning. You mainly feel the way you think. When
obnoxious and frustrating things happen to you at point
'A' (adversity), you consciously or unconsciously select
rational beliefs that lead you to feel concerned, sad and
remorseful and you also select irrational beliefs that lead
you to feel anxious, depressed and guilty.

▷ *Insight 2*: No matter how or when you acquired your
irrational beliefs and your self-sabotaging habits, you
now, in the present, choose to maintain them – and that
is why you are now disturbed. Your past history and your
present life conditions importantly affect you; but they
don't disturb you. Your present philosophy is the main
contributor to your current disturbance.

▷ *Insight 3*: There is no magical way for you to change your
strong tendencies needlessly to upset yourself. However,

you can minimize the impact of these tendencies through persistent work and practice to enable you to alter your irrational beliefs, your unhealthy feelings and your self-destructive behaviours.

8 Try to keep in touch with several other people who know something about REBT who can help go over some of its aspects with you. Tell them about problems that you have difficulty coping with and let them know how you are using REBT principles to overcome these problems. See if they agree with your solutions and ask them to suggest additional and better kinds of questioning methods that you can use to work against your irrational beliefs.

9 Practise using REBT methods with some of your friends, relatives and associates who are willing to let you try to help them with it. The more often you use it with others, and are able to see what their irrational beliefs are and to try to talk them out of these self-defeating ideas, the more you will be able to understand the main principles of REBT and to use them for yourself. When you see other people act irrationally and in a disturbed manner, try to figure out – with or without talking to them about it – what their main irrational beliefs probably are and how these could be actively and vigorously disputed.

10 Keep going back to REBT reading and audiovisual material from time to time, to keep reminding yourself of some of the main REBT principles and philosophies.

11 Remember and use the following philosophy concerning how to deal with obstacles to maintaining the gains you have made.

Insight

Perhaps the key to maintaining your gains is committing yourself to thinking rationally about adversities and acting and thinking in ways that are consistent with your rational beliefs when you encounter such adversities.

Develop and implement a philosophy of dealing with obstacles to maintaining your gains

In Chapter 14 I will consider the most common obstacles that people encounter as they strive to meet their personal goals. In this section

I want to stress the importance of developing and implementing a philosophy of dealing with obstacles to maintaining the gains you have made.

It would be nice to think that when you have made progress at achieving your personal goals, then you have done all the hard work that you need to do in the change process. Sadly, this is not the case. How many times have you succeeded at losing weight, for example, only to relax your efforts and put that weight back later? Mark Twain once said, 'Giving up smoking is easy, I've done it hundreds of times!' I have already pointed out that it is highly likely that you will experience lapses in your progress and, if you don't identify and deal effectively with your vulnerability factors, then you will increase your chances of relapsing.

When I talk of a philosophy of dealing with obstacles to maintaining the gains you have made, I mean the following:

- ▷ Recognize that you will continue to experience obstacles to maintaining the changes you have made throughout the change process.
- ▷ Refrain from demanding that this not be the case. Rather, accept, but do not like, this undesirable state of affairs.
- ▷ Resolve to use the 'Situational ABC' framework to assess obstacles to maintaining progress whenever you encounter them.
- ▷ Identify and examine any irrational beliefs that you discover which account for your obstacles.
- ▷ Construct, develop and rehearse rational alternatives to these irrational beliefs.
- ▷ Act and think in ways that are in keeping with these rational beliefs as you confront the obstacles at 'A'.
- ▷ Once you have done this go back to 'A' to re-examine it. If it is distorted, correct the distortion.
- ▷ Identify, challenge and change any core irrational beliefs that you hold which explain why you may perceive obstacles at 'A' that in reality are not there.
- ▷ Develop, rehearse and strengthen through action alternative core rational beliefs and see the effect that doing so has on the inferences that you make at 'A'.

▷ Make the practice of the self-help methods of REBT an integral part of your ongoing response to any obstacles that you encounter and of your future self-care regime.

Insight

Developing a philosophy of dealing with obstacles to maintaining your gains will help to deal with these obstacles when they arise.

In the following chapter I will discuss the issue of dealing with obstacles to change more broadly.

THINGS TO REMEMBER

▶ Once you have made gains, do not rest on your laurels. You need to take responsibility for actively working to maintain these gains.

▶ The key to maintaining your gains is to implement the idea that you need to keep thinking rationally about adversities and to keep acting and thinking in ways that are consistent with such rational thinking.

▶ Developing a philosophy of dealing with obstacles to maintaining your gains provides the foundation for actually dealing with them.

14

Dealing with obstacles to change

In this chapter you will learn:
- *about some of the obstacles to change that prevent you from identifying and responding to your irrational beliefs*
- *the powerful role that avoiding discomfort plays in obstacles to change*
- *that you may disturb yourself about your original disturbance and how this secondary disturbance may prevent you working on your original problem*
- *how to respond to all these obstacles and reservations so that you can deal effectively with your problems and become more emotionally healthy.*

In this chapter I will discuss some of the major obstacles within you that are manifested in the self-change process and how you can address these obstacles effectively.

You are reluctant to take responsibility

You are responsible for that which falls within your sphere of influence. So what is within your sphere of influence? In my view, thoughts, feelings and behaviours fall within your sphere of influence. However, you may find yourself echoing the wider society when you claim, for example, 'He made me feel anxious', 'She made me do it' and 'He put the idea into my head that I'm a failure'. How can you be responsible for what you clearly believe you are not responsible for or in control of? If you do not accept and practise emotional responsibility – i.e. you largely disturb yourself through the rigid and extreme beliefs that you hold about adversities at 'A' – then you are unlikely to use REBT to help yourself with your emotional problems.

Another reason why you might resist taking emotional responsibility is because you may equate it with blame: 'If I take responsibility for creating my feelings then I am stupid for doing so.' Rather than blame yourself it is easier not to accept responsibility. Here, it is important to distinguish between responsibility and blame: responsibility is acknowledging what is within your sphere of control (emotional reactions) without self-condemnation while blame is acknowledging what is within one's sphere of control with self-condemnation ('I'm weak and pathetic for getting angry'). So one way of taking emotional responsibility is not to blame yourself when you assume such responsibility.

Insight

If you don't take responsibility for disturbing yourself about the adversities you face, then, put simply, you won't change. Remember this point and fully accept that you disturb yourself about these adversities by the irrational beliefs that you hold about them.

You believe that change is not possible

You may have come to REBT quite discouraged about the possibility of achieving psychotherapeutic change. If you hold this idea, then you will only engage superficially in the process of REBT or not engage at all.

In dealing with the 'I can't change' obstacle, consider a time when you had the experience of personal change even though at the time you were sure you couldn't change. This will help you to at least consider the possibility that the same thing may happen again in REBT. If you have not had this experience, then ask yourself if you are, at least, prepared to try REBT with an open mind while not constantly rehearsing your 'I can't change' idea. If you are prepared to engage in REBT with an open mind, you will often find that you can experience some degree of personal change, and when this happens this is evidence against your 'I can't change' idea.

You think that you can't escape the past

You may believe that past events determine your present behaviour and feelings or have 'fixed' your character for ever – for example, your sibling may have died when you were very young and you conclude that your character has been defined irrevocably as a result. From this perspective, if you think that you can't escape your past, you may well have a pessimistic view of your ability to help yourself or believe that a long time needs to be spent exploring your troubled past if you are to make any progress. REBT argues, by contrast, that your current thinking about past events is largely responsible for your continuing disturbance about these events – you think about yourself today in the same way that you did in the past.

It is important that you distinguish between past events contributing to your current disturbance and these past events fixing for all time your disturbed response. Tough as it may seem to take, it is likely that many people had similar past experiences as you and probably had a variety of different responses. Consequently, it is not the event on its own that determines your disturbance, but the event plus your attitude towards it. It is true that you cannot change the past, but you can change your present attitude to the past. Have an open mind and see what happens if you work on changing your current beliefs about past events. You may be pleasantly surprised!

You think that the other person has to change

Another obstacle to change is when you think that the person about whom you are disturbed has to change first in order for you to get over your disturbance. When you insist that others have to change before you can start to feel better, this goal is outside of your control. Such a goal will keep you in a subordinate position in your relations with others as well as deprive you of the chance to develop emotional autonomy or regulation through changing your beliefs. If you believe that the other person has to change for you to get over your emotional problem, think of the likely consequences of tying your feelings to the other person's behaviour. It means that you have no control over your own feelings; all that control is in the hands of the other. But the truth is that *you* have given *them* that control. REBT says that, even if the other person's behaviour is very bad, then you still have the choice of having healthy negative feelings or unhealthy negative feelings about that behaviour and that you can change the latter to the former by changing your irrational beliefs about the other person's behaviour to rational beliefs.

Also it is important that you view the other person's bad behaviour within the context of the 'two principles of human interaction':

1 You get the behaviour you are prepared to tolerate without protest *and*
2 If we want to influence someone else's behaviour, it is important that you change your behaviour first.

The message of REBT is twofold:

1 Change yourself first before you attempt to change the other person.
2 The best chance that you have of influencing the other person to change is if you are not disturbed about that person's behaviour.

So rather than wait for the other person to change before you feel healthy, feel healthy before you attempt to effect change in the other's behaviour.

You opt for short-term 'solutions' to your problem

REBT basically proposes a long-term solution to your problems. As described throughout this book, this basically involves you identifying, questioning and changing the irrational beliefs that underpin your problems and thinking and acting in ways that strengthen your conviction in your developing rational beliefs. In REBT, belief change is the preferred form of therapeutic change, but there are other forms of personal change. So, if you can't change your beliefs at 'B' in the 'ABC' framework, you can make as constructive a change as possible (e.g. by changing your behaviour at 'C' or by modifying your inferences at 'A').

Before using REBT as outlined in this book, it is likely that you have tried to solve your problems in a number of ways which may have brought you short-term relief, but these 'solutions' have not, in fact, solved your problems, but have often unwittingly perpetuated them. One of the main tasks that you have in overcoming your obstacles to change is to discourage yourself from using these short-term 'solutions' to your problems. Here is a brief list of such 'solutions' and how to best tackle them.

DENIAL

You may try to help yourself deal with your emotional disturbance in the short-term by denying to yourself and/or others that you have problems. The best response to this is reflecting without shame on your present situation and, if necessary, to imagine that a loved one was in your situation and to consider how you would advise your loved one. Would you encourage this person to admit to her problems and commit herself to the helping process or would you encourage the person to say that she did not have problems? You would probably do the former.

Denial is also fuelled by shame. If you are ashamed of something then one way of dealing with it is to deny that it is a problem for you. Addressing your shame-fuelled self-depreciation belief helps you to admit to yourself that you have a problem.

OVERCOMPENSATION

You may attempt to deal with your problems in the short-term by overcompensating for them – i.e. by adopting a stance that is the very opposite to how you truly feel. Doing so helps you to feel good in the very short-term, but only serves to reinforce the irrational beliefs for which you are overcompensating. A common form of overcompensation is the adoption of a superior stance to cope with feelings of inferiority. In order to refrain from adopting an overcompensatory position and to deal with the irrational beliefs that underpin your problem you need to:

▶ understand the function of your overcompensatory stance and the irrational beliefs that they are meant to keep at bay
▶ construct alternative rational beliefs and a more functional behavioural and thinking alternative to the overcompensatory stance you have currently adopted
▶ see that the new rational beliefs and the more functional stance help you to achieve your goals and, by contrast, that your irrational beliefs and overcompensatory stance serve only to perpetuate your problem
▶ choose which path you wish to take (rational beliefs + non-compensatory stance v irrational beliefs + overcompensatory stance)
▶ tolerate the short-term discomfort that will ensue when you choose the former path over the latter
▶ adopt repeatedly the non-compensatory stance while rehearsing the rational beliefs that are consistent with it.

Safety-seeking behaviour is overt or covert behaviour that you perform to keep yourself, from your frame of reference, safe from threat in the short-term. Thus, a person who is scared of fainting in a supermarket may hold on to her friend to prevent herself from fainting. Safety-seeking behaviour has a similar function to overcompensatory behaviour and has similar poor long-term results. Consequently, a similar therapeutic approach to the one outlined above with respect to overcompensatory behaviour is called for with one addition – i.e. it is important for you to test out the validity of your thinking consequence at 'C'. Thus, at some point the woman discussed above needs to let go of her friend to see if she faints or not.

Behaviour change not in line with cognitive change

Behaviour that stems from irrational beliefs can easily become habitual and you may perform such behaviour even though you have challenged and begun to change your irrational beliefs. If this happens, you need to take the following steps:

▶ understand this phenomenon
▶ identify a functional alternative to this behaviour
▶ see that there is a difference between experiencing an urge to enact the habitual, but dysfunctional, behaviour (action tendency) and acting on this urge
▶ monitor and accept the existence of your urge to enact the dysfunctional behaviour
▶ see clearly that you have a choice – you can either act on this urge or act against this urge by enacting the functional alternative behaviour
▶ understand that doing the latter is far less familiar than the former and, if you choose the latter, you will experience the acute discomfort of acting unnaturally
▶ realize that doing this is in your best long-term interests and that you need to remind yourself of this fact when you make your choice as discussed above
▶ acknowledge that this discomfort lessens as you become more used to acting functionally.

You have reservations about your goals

I mentioned earlier in this book that it is important that you set goals for change. Doing so gives you a direction for self-therapy. There are three types of goals that are linked together: emotional goals, behavioural goals and thinking goals. Thus, if a person is anxious about asking women to dance and therefore avoids doing so:

▶ his emotional goal would be to feel concerned rather than anxious about being turned down
▶ his behavioural goal would be to ask women out rather than avoid doing so, *and*
▶ his thinking goal would be to recognize that, of a number of women that he asks to dance, some will dance with him and others will not, rather than thinking that nobody will dance with him.

You might think that setting these goals is straightforward and that you will be clearly committed to goals that are so clearly healthier for you than your currently experienced problems. Often this is the case, but not always. Sometimes you may have reservations about the goals you have set and this becomes apparent when you notice that you have made less progress towards your goals than you might realistically expect.

There are two major occasions when it is useful to check for possible reservations that you may hold about your set goals. The first occasion is when you first set them. Asking yourself such questions as 'What negative consequences, if any, might I encounter if I achieve my goals?', 'What would I lose, if anything, if I were to achieve my goals?', 'Do I anticipate any problems working towards my goals?' helps to stimulate your thinking on this issue. You may also do a more formal cost–benefit analysis on your problems and goals to assess more fully your reservations about your goals and the process of working towards them. A typical cost–benefit analysis form asks you to list both the advantages/benefits and the disadvantages/costs of a) your problem and, separately, b) your goal from a short-term and from a long-term perspective and as experienced by yourself and relevant others. The information that you get from this form often alerts you to potential future reservations that you may have about your goal if none are currently apparent.

The second major occasion to check whether or not you have reservations about your goals is when it becomes clear that you are not working towards them as diligently as you might expect.

Of course, there may be many reasons why you may not be working towards your goals other than goal-related reservations, many of which I will discuss later in this chapter. When you suspect that you are encountering an obstacle to change, then you should, at the very least, consider that this may be due to your reservations about your stated goals and you should review your goals as well as any reservations that you might have about them. In this respect, it is important to note that your goals do change over time and, consequently, don't expect that the goals that you set at the beginning of self-therapy will remain unchanged throughout the process of REBT.

You expect more than questioning irrational beliefs can deliver

If you expect your longstanding and often tenaciously held irrational beliefs to crumble immediately in the face of your questioning and emerging rational beliefs, you will be disappointed. Thus, you might say: 'I keep on telling myself that I'm a fallible human being who has had failures in his life but I'm not a failure, but I just don't believe it.' You may only recently have learned to separate your actions from yourself – to judge the former but not the latter – and your irrational belief that actions do define your character still remains much more credible to you. If you think that questioning beliefs should not result in continuing tension and conflict between old and new beliefs, you are expecting unrealistic results from such questioning as such tension is almost inevitable. Your view will lead you to stop such questioning prematurely, with the consequence that you will return to your well-established irrational beliefs.

It is important that you realize that belief change involves going over many times the evidence for and the benefits of the new belief and the lack of evidence for and costs of adhering to the old belief. It is also important that you spend more time on building up the new belief rather than revisiting the old one. As well as this cognitive examination, it is crucial that you repeatedly and forcefully act in support of your new developing rational belief and against your more established irrational belief. Unless you act on what you know you won't develop conviction in what you know.

You have reservations about rational beliefs

As we have seen, one of your major tasks in using REBT is to achieve your goals by identifying and questioning your irrational beliefs and changing them to their healthy rational equivalents. In doing so, it is important that you see clearly that your rational beliefs can help you to achieve your goals. Unless you see this, you may not be motivated to acquire these rational beliefs. However, even though you may see this rational belief–goals connection, you may still resist change because you may have reservations about adopting the rational beliefs.

The following are typical reservations that people hold about flexible beliefs, non-awfulizing beliefs, discomfort tolerance beliefs and self- and other- and life-acceptance beliefs. I will also show you how to respond to them once you have uncovered any that are relevant to you.

FLEXIBLE BELIEFS LEAD TO DECREASED MOTIVATION TO REACH GOALS AND TO LESSER EFFORT

Here, you consider that 'musts' both enhance motivation and lead to increased effort and that, by contrast, your flexible preferences are diluting your motivation to achieve prized goals and lead to lesser effort. For example, Keith argued that adopting the flexible belief 'I want to do well in my forthcoming examination, but I don't have to do so' would mean that he wouldn't study as hard as he would if he kept his demand: 'I must do well in my forthcoming examination.' Since Keith wants to study hard, he is likely to resist adopting this rational belief as long as he sees it interfering with his motivation to study and the effort that he would put in while studying.

Response
Here, you need to understand that flexible beliefs do not preclude strong motivation and determined effort to achieve valued objectives. It is true, for example, that Keith's rigid demand may lead him to study hard for his exam, but his study may well be punctuated with increased anxiety and task-irrelevant thinking that will probably interfere with the efficiency of his studying. In this respect, Keith's demand may also prevent him from taking healthy breaks from studying and lead him to become overly tired – a state which is conducive neither to good study habits nor to optimal examination performance. By contrast, Keith's flexible belief will increase the efficiency of his studying by helping him to focus on the content of

what he is revising rather than on the task-irrelevant thoughts that stem from his rigid demand and will encourage him to take breaks from study which will help him to stay fresh and appropriately aroused for the examination itself.

NON-AWFULIZING BELIEFS MINIMIZE THE BADNESS OF VERY AVERSIVE NEGATIVE EVENTS

Here, you consider that an awfulizing belief accurately describes the full aversive nature of the very negative event about which you are disturbed and you view the alternative non-awfulizing belief as minimizing the badness of this event. For example, Graham argued that adopting the non-awfulizing belief 'It would be very bad if my wife were to leave me, but it wouldn't be the end of the world' would mean viewing this event as slightly bad or moderately bad. As a result, he resisted adopting this idea.

Response
Here, you need to see that adopting non-awfulizing beliefs does not preclude you from seeing personal tragedies as personal tragedies and catastrophes as catastrophes. Recently, an advertisement for an insurance company contained the slogan 'We won't make a drama out of a crisis.' The implication here was that the company would still respond to the crisis. REBT has a similar message. Effectively, it urges you to take the horror out of a crisis, but still to view a highly aversive event as a crisis and to respond to it as such. Thus, Graham who thought that the above-mentioned non-awfulizing belief minimized the badness of his wife leaving him eventually saw that holding this belief meant that this would be a tragedy for him, but like other people he could learn to transcend this personal tragedy, which he could not do if his wife leaving him were truly awful. Once you define something as awful, you are implying that you cannot transcend the experience, no matter how you think about it. In making this distinction, Graham saw that by viewing his wife leaving him as a personal tragedy, but not awful, he neither minimized nor exaggerated the badness of the event. Rather, he acknowledged it for what it is: a personal tragedy.

NON-AWFULIZING BELIEFS CONDONE OTHERS' BAD BEHAVIOUR

Here, you consider that a non-awfulizing belief condones the bad behaviour of another person whereas the awfulizing belief does not condone it. Thus, Karen argued that adopting the non-awfulizing belief 'It was very bad that my father left the family when I was young, but it was not the end of the world' would mean that she would be condoning his behaviour. As such, she resisted adopting this rational belief.

Response
In rebutting this reservation, it is important that you see the important difference between condoning something and holding a non-awfulizing belief about it. To condone another's bad behaviour means to absolve or to excuse the person for his behaviour. You do not do this when you hold a non-awfulizing belief about this behaviour. Rather, you hold the other fully responsible for his behaviour, asserting that it was very bad for him to act that way, while contradicting the idea that it was the end of the world that he acted very poorly. Thus, Karen needs to see that it was very bad, but not awful, for her father to leave his family when he did and that he needs to be held to account for his behaviour and that understanding why he did it is not tantamount to absolving him of this responsibility.

DISCOMFORT TOLERANCE BELIEFS DISCOURAGE YOU FROM CHANGING NEGATIVE EVENTS

Here, you consider that being encouraged to tolerate negative events means that you should grin and bear it, which means that you should take no action to change such events. Thus, Barbara argued that holding the discomfort tolerance belief 'It is hard to tolerate being criticized unfairly, but I can tolerate it' would mean that she should just put up with unfair criticism without doing anything about it. As such, she resisted adopting this belief.

Response
In rebutting this reservation, you need to see that far from leading to resignation, a discomfort tolerance belief helps you to change a negative event effectively by encouraging you to think clearly and objectively about how you can best respond to the negative event in question. By contrast, the alternative discomfort intolerance belief leads to impulsive, non-reflective behaviour which decreases the chances that you will respond effectively to the negative event. Thus, it is important for Barbara to see that developing tolerance of criticism enables her to think about how to answer the unfair

criticism and thus respond effectively to the person making it. It does not mean suffering in silence in the face of such criticism, nor does it mean lashing out at the other person (a response more characteristic of a discomfort intolerance belief).

SELF-ACCEPTANCE BELIEFS ENCOURAGE RESIGNATION OR COMPLACENCY

Here you think that the term 'acceptance' either means that you have to resign yourself to the way that you are and that change is not possible or it encourages complacency in that, although change is possible, there is no need to change because you are OK the way you are. As a consequence, you resist the idea of self-acceptance.

Response
In dealing with these reservations, it is important for you to see exactly what self-acceptance means from an REBT perspective. In this context, it means acknowledging that you are a complex being comprising many different aspects – positive, negative and neutral. Thus, it is certainly possible for you to accept the whole of you and still recognize that you have negative aspects of yourself that can be changed. Thus, self-acceptance does not mean self-resignation nor does it encourage complacency. Indeed, because an attitude of self-acceptance minimizes psychological disturbance, this attitude promotes change because it enables you to devote your energies to focusing on what you don't like about yourself, to understanding the factors that are involved with such aspects and to intervening productively on these factors. Lack of self-acceptance leads to disturbed feelings and thus diverts your energies away from constructive self-change.

> **Insight**
> Just because a belief is deemed rational by REBT does not mean that you will embrace it without qualification. Indeed, you may have reservations about surrendering irrational beliefs and adopting rational beliefs. Identify such reservations and respond to them as persuasively as you can.

You think that insight is enough

Many people believe that, when they understand the factors that account for the existence of their psychological problems and what they need to do to deal with these factors, then this insight leads to psychotherapeutic change. If only this was the case. If you ascribe to this view, then you need to see more clearly the difference between intellectual insight and emotional insight. From an REBT perspective, when you have intellectual insight, you have a cognitive understanding of the following:

▶ that irrational beliefs underpin your psychological problems
▶ that the alternatives to these irrational beliefs are rational beliefs and that holding rational beliefs represents the most stable way of overcoming your problems
▶ that you need to question your irrational beliefs and see that they are false and illogical and have largely dysfunctional consequences
▶ that you need to question your rational beliefs and see that they are true and logical and have largely functional consequences
▶ that you need to question both sets of beliefs many times before you begin to truly believe your rational beliefs and disbelieve your irrational beliefs
▶ that you need to act and think in ways that are consistent with your developing rational beliefs and do so repeatedly while facing relevant 'As'
▶ that while facing these 'As' you need to refrain from acting and thinking in ways that are consistent with the irrational beliefs that you wish to disbelieve.

Intellectual insight can be gained from books and does not lead to enduring psychotherapeutic change because it does not involve you doing anything to change. Thus, when you have intellectual insight you may understand, for example, that demanding that your boss like you is irrational, but you still have the dysfunctional effects of holding this belief. You may further understand that believing that you do not need your boss to like you is rational, but you do not realize the true emotive, behavioural and cognitive benefits of this rational belief.

Emotional insight, on the other hand, can be gained only by putting into practice intellectual insight and doing so regularly and with commitment and energy. This form of insight cannot be derived from books. In short, if you believe that intellectual insight is sufficient to promote psychotherapeutic change, it is important to disabuse yourself of this idea.

You believe that change is too hard

If you think that personal change is too hard, you need to understand what you think is 'too hard' about the change process and address the issue accordingly as shown below.

▶ You may have unrealistic expectations that change would be relatively smooth and painless. If so, revise your expectations so that change is now based on the maxim 'There's no gain without some pain.'

▶ Unanticipated problem areas in your life have emerged adding considerably to the list of problems that you need to deal with. If so, realize that an increased problem list does not have to be an overwhelming one. What may appear to be a 'mass' of problems are usually linked by two or three key irrational beliefs. Change these beliefs and the number of problems shrinks.

▶ The changes that you have made have provoked unfavourable reactions from others (e.g. family, friends, colleagues) that you find difficult to cope with. If this is the case, you might be expecting too much support or understanding from others without realizing that your changes are provoking changes in them which may be unwanted or uncomfortable for them. Instead of brooding on these unfavourable reactions, you can come up with ways of better managing them (e.g. 'I know and accept that my husband does not want to pull his weight helping around the house, but that's not going to stop me prodding him to do his share'). However, sometimes you may have to accept the grim conclusion that you have to 'go it alone' if you want to achieve your goals.

▶ You may think that you are losing your identity because of the strange, unfamiliar thoughts and feelings you are experiencing. If this is the case, realize that the fear of losing your identity is based on the false notion that the self is defined by an aspect of it (e.g. 'I've always been an impulsive, driven person. I won't know who I am if I start to act in a calmer manner, even though I know it would be better for my health'). This simple view of the self – a few traits define you – can be replaced by a complex view of the self – i.e. that it is unrateable. Would you lose your identity if you were required to change from being right-handed to left-handed? Of course not. This means that you lose your identity only if you define it narrowly.

▶ You think that you are making such little progress that you despair of ever seeing light at the end of the tunnel. Not seeing light at the end of the tunnel may occur because you are demanding immediate progress, you are dithering about at the entrance to the tunnel rather than entering it (i.e. you keep talking about change instead of implementing it) or you are moving so slowly along the tunnel to keep within your comfort zone that every step is 'agonizing'. Light at the end of the tunnel will be seen relatively quickly if you commit yourself to change, make the effort associated with it and then move purposefully down the tunnel.

You are not prepared to work for change

You may understand the concept of self-help, but you are not prepared to act on it. There may be a number of reasons for your refusal to work for change. The following three reasons are typical.

'I DON'T HAVE THE TIME TO CARRY OUT SELF-HELP ASSIGNMENTS'

You may have a very busy lifestyle that may or may not reflect your psychological problems. The last thing you want under these circumstances is more work and thus you may very well baulk at the idea of carrying out self-help assignments because you see these assignments as adding to your burden. In this case, view these self-help assignments as something you can do at spare moments such as while having breakfast or while on train journeys to and from work. I usually state that, because of my other commitments, I do not write in large time blocks but in ten-minute periods here and there. It is amazing how much you can get done if you utilize small time periods.

'I SHOULDN'T HAVE TO CARRY OUT SELF-HELP ASSIGNMENTS'

You may think that, because you have a lot on in life or for other reasons, you shouldn't have to carry out self-help assignments. In reality, of course, you will only reap therapeutically what you are prepared to sow in terms of doing self-help assignments. Thus, it is important that you challenge your idea that you shouldn't have to do homework assignments. The best way to do this is to use behavioural experiments rather than cognitive arguments. First, realize that you may be correct in assuming that you may benefit from REBT without doing homework assignments. Be prepared to be open-minded about this by putting this idea to the test. For an agreed period don't do any self-help assignments and then for an equivalent period do such assignments. Then, at the end of this experiment, evaluate the results. If you conduct the experiment properly you may well conclude that you derived more benefit from doing self-help assignments than from not doing them. If the results are otherwise, then don't do any self-help assignments.

'I'M TOO LAZY'

You may refuse to carry out self-help assignments because you claim to be too lazy to do anything to help yourself. This self-description, of course, demonstrates a philosophy of discomfort intolerance and people who describe themselves as such have problems underpinned by the same philosophy. They literally bring this philosophy to therapy.

The way to deal with this major obstacle to change is twofold. First, it is important to dis-identify with your so-called 'laziness'. See that you are not a lazy person, but a person who holds a set of beliefs that lead to you not being prepared to take constructive action on your own behalf. Such dis-identification encourages you to see that you do not have to change your identity to help yourself overcome your problems, only some of your beliefs.

Second, understand that when you hold a discomfort intolerance belief about doing a self-help assignment, you think that doing the assignment will be far more uncomfortable than if you hold a discomfort tolerance belief about doing the same assignment. Having overestimated the discomfort you will experience, realize that you will then avoid doing the assignment. After you understand this dynamic, conduct a behavioural experiment where you first undertake to carry out a self-help assignment while holding a discomfort intolerance belief and then do one while holding a discomfort tolerance belief. This should help you to see that you construct greater discomfort in your mind than exists in reality.

You are intolerant of the discomfort and unfamiliarity of change

A particular set of discomfort intolerance beliefs constitutes a frequently encountered obstacle to psychotherapeutic change. The object of this set of beliefs is change itself; sometimes it is the discomfort that you experience when you begin to change and at other times it is the sense of unfamiliarity that change brings. When you begin to change, you will feel uncomfortable since this is an inevitable feature of psychotherapeutic change. If you believe that you must not experience this discomfort then you will stop working to achieve your goals and will likely stop changing. In such a case, it is important that you see that:

▶ Discomfort is an inevitable part of change.
▶ Change-related discomfort can be tolerated and if you keep your goals clearly in mind then it can be seen that such discomfort is worth tolerating in that it aids goal attainment.
▶ Holding a discomfort intolerance belief about change-related discomfort leads to the prediction of greater discomfort than does holding a discomfort tolerance belief.
▶ Continuing to act and think in ways that are consistent with developing rational beliefs will lead to a decrease of change-related discomfort.

If you act on these four insights then you will be well on the way to overcoming this obstacle to psychotherapeutic change.

When you begin to change, you will experience a sense of unfamiliarity. As I often say: 'If it ain't strange, it ain't change.' If you believe that you can't bear this unfamiliarity then you will engineer things so that you will return to the uncomfortable but familiar state of your problems. Helping yourself deal with this obstacle is similar to helping yourself to deal with the obstacle of change-related discomfort. Thus, you need to see that:

▶ Unfamiliarity is an inevitable part of change.
▶ A sense of change-related unfamiliarity can be tolerated and if you keep your goals clearly in mind then it can be seen that such unfamiliarity is worth tolerating in that it aids goal attainment.

- Holding a discomfort intolerance belief about a sense of change-related unfamiliarity leads to the prediction of a greater sense of unfamiliarity than does holding a discomfort tolerance belief.
- Continuing to act and think in ways that are consistent with developing rational beliefs will lead to a decrease of change-related unfamiliarity and eventually a new sense of familiarity.

Insight

Change involves both much effort and tolerating discomfort. If you are prepared to do both then you will change. If you are not, you won't.

You have a meta-emotional problem which you don't deal with

People often have meta-emotional problems about their original emotional problems (e.g. anger about feeling depressed). A meta-emotional problem is literally an emotional problem that you have about your original emotional problem. When you disturb yourself about the problem that you have targeted to change then you may not work on this original problem very effectively since you are disturbed about it. As a result, you will not make much progress on your original problem and your meta-emotional problem serves as an obstacle to you doing so.

So what can you do? You need to determine if you have a meta-emotional problem. For example, if your original problem is anxiety, ask yourself 'How do I feel about feeling anxious?' to determine whether you do, in fact, have a meta-emotional problem about your original problem of anxiety. If you do, you will commonly experience anxiety, depression, shame, unhealthy anger (usually at yourself) and guilt, and consequently you need to use the following guidelines.

KNOW WHEN TO WORK ON THE META-EMOTIONAL PROBLEM FIRST

If either of the following two conditions are met, I suggest that you target your meta-emotional problem for change first:

1 Your meta-emotional problem interferes significantly with the work you are trying to do on your original problem.

2 You can see the sense of working on your meta-emotional problem first.

In effect, here your meta-emotional problem effectively becomes your target problem and you deal with it by following exactly the same steps as you would if your original problem was your target problem.

THINGS TO REMEMBER

You can overcome your obstacles to change if you do the following:

▶ Take responsibility for disturbing yourself.

▶ Realize that while change is difficult, it is possible.

▶ Realize that while your past influences your current problems, it does not cause them.

▶ If your problems are with others, accept that you need to change rather than wait for them to change.

▶ Resist taking short-term solutions to your problems designed to help you to feel better. Your task is to get better in the long-term rather than to feel better in the short-term.

▶ Identify and respond to your reservations about your goals for change.

▶ Be realistic about what you can derive from cognitive questioning of your irrational beliefs.

▶ Understand that such questioning is a prelude to taking action based on your developing rational beliefs.

▶ Identify and respond to your reservations about your rational beliefs. Realize that such reservations are frequently based on misconceptions about the true nature of these rational beliefs.

▶ Realize that there are two forms of insight in REBT: *intellectual* and *emotional*. See that change comes about from gaining emotional insight. This involves repeatedly acting and thinking in ways that are consistent with your rational beliefs. If you implement this point you will change. If you don't you won't.

▶ Accept that, while making changes is hard, it is not too hard.

▶ Accept that change comes about through hard work.

▶ Be prepared to tolerate the discomfort and unfamiliarity of change.

▶ Identify and work on any meta-emotional problem you have which is preventing you from working effectively on your original problem.

15

Dealing with anxiety

In this chapter you will learn:
- *what we generally get anxious about*
- *the healthy alternative to anxiety*
- *the important role that beliefs play in determining anxiety and its healthy alternative*
- *the role that safety-seeking measures play in the maintenance of anxiety*
- *a step-by-step guide to assessing and dealing with specific instances of anxiety*
- *how to deal with anxiety in general as well as in particular*
- *the importance of developing a healthy attitude to anxiety.*

When you experience anxiety (or its healthy alternative, concern), you are facing or think you are facing some kind of threat. This is true as long as your anxiety is psychologically based. There are some medical conditions where you experience anxiety and, if you routinely cannot point to some kind of threat when you are anxious, it is probably best to rule out a medical cause before assuming that your anxiety is psychological in origin. In such cases a visit to your GP/family doctor is in order. However, let's assume in this chapter that there is nothing medically wrong with you and that your anxiety is psychologically based.

Understanding threat

In order to understand the nature of threat, you need to understand a concept known as the 'personal domain'.

THE PERSONAL DOMAIN

Dr Aaron T. Beck, one of the founding fathers of CBT, introduced the concept of the 'personal domain' which I have found very useful in helping people understand their emotions (Beck 1976). The personal domain refers to the people, concepts, values and objects that are important to us. These people etc. can occupy a central, intermediate or peripheral place in our personal domain.

As I said earlier, we experience anxiety when we face or think we are facing a threat to someone or something within our personal domain. The more central a place that the person or thing occupies, the more anxious we will feel. However, threat on its own does not explain whether we feel anxiety or its healthy alternative, concern. The REBT model that I discussed in Chapter 2 holds that the main determinant of anxiety is the set of irrational beliefs that we hold at 'B' about the threat at 'A'.

DIFFERENT THREATS ARE ASSOCIATED WITH DIFFERENT TYPES OF ANXIETY

What we find threatening suggests the type of anxiety we are likely to experience. Thus, if you experience social anxiety, the threat is that you may act inappropriately in public and that others will evaluate you negatively if you do so. In health anxiety, you find uncertainty about the status of your health threatening, while in panic disorder you find threats to your self-control particularly difficult. However, it is important to reiterate that these threats at 'A', on their own, only explain that you will experience anxiety or concern. They do not help you to tell which of these two emotions you will actually experience.

Insight
In psychologically based anxiety, no threat, no anxiety (or concern). However, when you perceive threat you feel anxious because you hold irrational beliefs about it and you feel concerned because you hold rational beliefs about it.

Understanding anxiety by using the 'ABC' framework

You can best understand anxiety by using the 'ABC' framework. In what follows, I will present in general terms an 'ABC' formulation of anxiety (see Table 15.1) and an 'ABC' formulation of concern (the healthy alternative to anxiety) (see Table 15.2).

What these two tables show is that you can distinguish between anxiety and concern, not only by your beliefs (irrational in the former and rational in the latter), but also by considering what you do (or feel like doing) and how you think when you feel anxious.

Thus, when you hold an irrational belief about a threat to your personal domain you will tend to seek safety while at the same time exaggerating the nature of the threat and underestimating your ability to cope with it.

Table 15.1 'ABC' formulation of anxiety.

'A'	▶ Threat
'B'	▶ You hold irrational beliefs about the threat
'C' (emotional)	▶ Anxiety
'C' (behavioural) [Overt behaviour or action tendencies]	▶ You avoid the threat ▶ You withdraw from the threat ▶ You make wide use of behavioural safety-seeking measures in the presence of the threat
'C' (thinking)	▶ You exaggerate the nature of the threat ▶ You have a highly distorted and negative view of the consequences of the threat ▶ You see yourself as being unable to cope with the threat ▶ You make wide use of cognitive safety-seeking measures in the presence of the threat

Table 15.2 'ABC' formulation of concern.

'A'	▶ Threat
'B'	▶ You hold rational beliefs about the threat

'C' (emotional)	▶ Concern
'C' (behavioural) [Overt behaviour or action tendencies]	▶ You face the threat ▶ You attempt to deal with the threat ▶ You make sparing use of behavioural safety-seeking measures in the presence of the threat
'C' (thinking)	▶ You have a realistic view of the nature of the threat ▶ You have a realistic and balanced view of the consequences of the threat ▶ You see yourself as being able to cope with the threat ▶ You make sparing use of cognitive safety-seeking measures in the presence of the threat

Dealing with anxiety: overview

The above analysis suggests that to deal with your anxiety you need to do the following:

1 Replace your irrational belief with its rational alternative.
2 Face the threat and deal with it rather than seek safety from it.
3 View the threat realistically rather than exaggerate its nature.
4 Reconsider your ability to cope with the threat.

In REBT, we say that you need to take step number one first (i.e. replace your irrational belief with its rational belief alternative) and then take the remaining steps in the order that you think will help you the most. However, if you want to deal with anxiety in a comprehensive manner you do need to take all four steps.

Insight

The key to feeling concerned rather than anxious about a threat is to hold rational beliefs about the threat. But these beliefs will only take hold when you act and think in ways that are consistent with them.

Dealing with anxiety: a specific example

In this section I will discuss how one person, Joanne, dealt with a specific example of her anxiety. I will then outline the steps that you need to take to do the same with a specific example of your own anxiety.

Joanne experiences anxiety in formal social settings which she usually avoids. However, her boss has asked her to accompany him to the firm's annual dinner and she cannot get out of attending. She first uses the 'Situational ABC' framework to assess her problem.

USING THE 'SITUATIONAL ABC' FRAMEWORK TO ASSESS AND DEAL WITH A SPECIFIC EXAMPLE OF ANXIETY

In the steps that follow, Steps 1–5 outline what Joanne did to assess her chosen example of her social anxiety.

Step 1: Describe the situation
Joanne described the following situation in which she anticipates experiencing her problem:

> *'Sitting at the dinner table at the firm's annual dinner.'*

Step 2: Identify the unhealthy negative emotion in the situation (emotional 'C')
Joanne identified her problematic emotion as follows:

> *'Anxiety'*

Step 3: How I act and think when I feel anxious (behavioural 'C' and thinking 'C')
Joanne identified the behavioural 'C' and thinking 'C' that accompany her anxiety. This helped Joanne to know that she experienced anxiety rather than concern.

> *'When I feel anxious, I anticipate thinking that if I do anything inappropriate then everyone will notice and judge me negatively. I will therefore say nothing, but wish that I could escape.'*

Step 4: What I am most anxious about in the situation at 'A'
Joanne identified her 'A' as follows:

> *'I am most anxious about saying or doing something inappropriate at the formal dinner.'*

Please note that, according to standard REBT practice, Joanne assumed temporarily that she would say or do something inappropriate at the dinner. She will have a chance to examine this inference later once she has got herself into a rational frame of mind.

Step 5: What is my rigid belief and main extreme belief at B that accounts for my anxiety

Joanne identified her two irrational beliefs as follows:

> '*I must not say or do anything inappropriate and it would be terrible if I do.*'

In Steps 6 and 7, Joanne outlines what would constitute a healthier way of dealing with the threat. Note that she formulates alternative rational beliefs and specifies how these would lead to a very different set of consequences for her.

Step 6: Formulating alternative rational beliefs

It is important that Joanne formulates rational alternatives to her irrational beliefs before she begins to question them. Otherwise, she may wish to give up her irrational beliefs, but have nothing to take their place.

Joanne formulated the following rational beliefs as alternatives to her rigid belief and awfulizing belief:

> '*I would prefer it if I do not say or do anything inappropriate, but it doesn't follow that I must not do so. If I do it would be bad, but not terrible.*'

Step 7: Specifying goals (the healthy alternatives to anxiety and the behaviour and thinking that accompany it)

The purpose of using REBT with your problems is to respond to adversities in a healthy manner with respect to your feelings and the behaviour and thinking that accompany them. These are the goals that you are aiming for. They are also the consequences of holding the rational beliefs that you formulated in Step 6. It follows that you need to be clear with yourself what these goals are.

Joanne specified her emotional, behavioural and thinking goals as follows:

> '*I am aiming to feel concerned but not anxious about saying or doing anything inappropriate in the situation, and to think that*

if I do then some people might notice and judge me negatively, but most probably won't. I am also aiming to speak up and enjoy myself as best I can.'

Step 8: Questioning beliefs

As discussed in Chapter 7, the purpose of questioning beliefs is for you to understand the irrationality of irrational beliefs and the rationality of your rational beliefs. This provides the platform for the behaviour and the thinking that you need to subsequently engage in to help you address your anxiety effectively.

Joanne wrote down her irrational beliefs and rational beliefs side by side and using the arguments discussed in Chapter 7 showed herself that her rational beliefs were true, logical and helpful and that her irrational beliefs were false, illogical and unhelpful.

'I can see that it is always possible for me to say something inappropriate at the dinner and for me to demand that I must not do so does not remove the possibility. Indeed, this demand may even increase the possibility that I may say something inappropriate because it leads to me being very anxious which in turn interferes with me being able to concentrate on the conversations.

'However, it is true that I would prefer it if I did not say something inappropriate, and it is also true that I don't have to be immune from doing so. Also, while it would be unfortunate if I said something inappropriate, it is hardly awful if I do so. There are far worse things that could happen to people, so I am going to view it within a much wider framework.'

Step 9: Identifying behavioural and cognitive safety-seeking measures and their healthy alternatives

A major reason why people do not benefit from facing threat, even though we know that facing threat is the best way to deal with anxiety, is that they use a range of measures that are designed to keep them safe in the situation. The effect of using these safety-seeking measures is that you do not get to face the threat head on and therefore you never really experience the benefits that *in vivo* exposure will give you.

Safety-seeking measures are usually behavioural or cognitive in nature, although these are frequently employed together. It is important to identify them and to construct productive alternatives before facing the threat in reality or in imagination. I discuss this topic in greater detail later in the chapter and provide some examples (see 'Dealing with anxiety: from the specific to the general'). At this point I suggest that you:

▶ Make a list of safety-seeking measures that you would tend to use both in the situation and afterwards, were you to face the threat while holding your irrational beliefs. As I said above, these safety-seeking measures may be behavioural (what you do in the situation to keep yourself safe) or cognitive (what you think in the situation to keep yourself safe).

▶ For every safety-seeking measure identify a healthy alternative that enables you to face the threat and use your rational beliefs.

Joanne identified the following safety-seeking measures that she would be tempted to use in the situation and the healthy alternatives to these measures:

Behavioural safety-seeking measures	Healthy alternatives
Agreeing with people	Speaking my mind
Going to the toilet when feeling uncomfortable	Staying at the table when feeling uncomfortable

Cognitive safety-seeking measures	Healthy alternatives
Distracting myself when feeling uncomfortable	Acknowledging and accepting my discomfort
Rehearsing everything that I plan to say so that I don't sound stupid	Saying what I want to say without mentally rehearsing it first

Insight

It is natural to seek safety when you experience a threat. But if you want to deal effectively with your anxiety problem you have to go against this natural tendency and face the threat while using the tools of rational thinking rather than using your safety-seeking measures.

Step 10: Facing the specific threat in imagination while mentally rehearsing rational beliefs and acting and thinking accordingly
Perhaps the most important ingredient in dealing effectively with anxiety is to face what you find threatening armed with your new

rational beliefs. While it is best to do this in actual real-life situations, you may also gain benefit from facing your threat in your imagination. You can use imagery exposure (as it is called) under two conditions:

1 if it is not practical for you to face your threat in reality
2 as a preparation stage before you face your threat in reality.

When you use imagery exposure, I suggest that you follow these guidelines.

1 Focus on what you find threatening in your mind's eye. This is your 'A'.
2 Briefly allow yourself to experience your anxiety. I suggest this because it is a realistic scenario and shows that you can use this feeling as a cue to dealing with the feeling as discussed in the next guideline.
3 Use this feeling as a cue to rehearse your rational belief as you see yourself facing your threat and being realistic in your thinking about its consequences.
4 Hold this image until your feeling changes from anxiety to concern.
5 Make sure that you don't use any of the behavioural or cognitive safety-seeking measures that you identified in Step 9.

Here is Joanne's report of how she used imagery exposure:

'I focused on speaking up at the dinner and on the possibility that I might say something inappropriate until I experienced feelings of anxiety. I then used this as a cue to rehearse my rational belief (i.e. "I would prefer it if I do not say or do anything inappropriate, but it doesn't follow that I must not do so. If I do it would be bad, but not terrible"). I saw myself feeling concerned rather than anxious, which helped me to speak up. In doing so, I reminded myself that, if I did say something inappropriate, some people would notice and judge me negatively, but most probably wouldn't.'

A NOTE OF CAUTION
Let me add a note of caution here. A person may take a realistic and balanced thinking consequence of a rational belief (such as 'If I say or do something inappropriate then some people will notice and judge me, but most probably won't') and use it as a self-reassurance strategy to keep herself safe from the threat. If you do so, this is probably evidence that you are still holding on to your irrational

beliefs, rather than dealing effectively with the threat by developing your rational belief. You can tell that you are doing this if:

▶ when using imagery exposure you repeatedly try to convince yourself that most people probably won't notice your inappropriate behaviour and won't judge you for it. It is the repetition here that is indicative of safety-seeking rather than realistic and balanced thinking
▶ you focus on convincing yourself that most people probably won't notice and judge you for your inappropriate behaviour rather than on changing your irrational beliefs and developing the rational alternatives to these beliefs.

If Joanne misused the thinking consequences of her rational belief as a self-reassurance strategy then in practising imagery exposure I would suggest that she concentrate on seeing herself speak up and on rehearsing her rational belief and omit focusing on the realistic and balanced conclusion of this rational belief.

Please note one other point about using imagery exposure. It may be that the threat that you are attempting to face in your mind's eye is just too anxiety-provoking for you at that time. If that is the case, I suggest that you use a principle that I call 'challenging but not overwhelming'. Here, you use imagery to face a threat that you find challenging at the time, but not overwhelming. This principle also states that there is little therapeutic value in facing in your mind's eye something that you find minimally threatening.

Step 11: Facing the specific threat in reality while mentally rehearsing rational beliefs and acting and thinking accordingly

While imagery exposure has its place in helping you to deal effectively with anxiety as discussed above, it is important, whenever possible, for you to face specific threat in reality. This is called *in vivo* exposure as opposed to imagery exposure.

Implement the following principles when using *in vivo* exposure:

▶ Face your 'A' in reality. Use the 'challenging, but not overwhelming' principle (discussed above), if relevant.
▶ Rehearse your rational beliefs as you face your 'A'.
▶ Notice your tendency to use any of the safety-seeking measures you identified above. Instead, use in actuality the healthy alternative to the safety-seeking measure.

▶ Remind yourself of the realistic and balanced consequence of your rational belief without using it as a self-reassurance strategy (see above).

Joanne's report continues:

'I went to the dinner and faced my fear by speaking up at the dinner table, disagreeing several times with people who expressed views contrary to my own.

'While doing this, I rehearsed my rational belief that, while I would prefer not to say anything inappropriate, sadly I am not immune from doing so nor do I have to be immune. If I did say anything inappropriate, that would be nasty, but it would not be the end of the universe. I noticed when I was tempted to use safety-seeking behaviour and thinking, but used my healthy behavioural and thinking alternatives instead.

'Finally, I reminded myself that even if I did act inappropriately, most others would probably not notice my behaviour. This helped me to focus on engaging in conversation with people rather than on what they might be thinking about me.'

Step 12: Coming back to 'A'

In REBT, we recommend that you initially assume that 'A' is true temporarily (see Step 4) and that the best time to come back to 'A' to re-evaluate it is when you have got yourself into a rational frame of mind (see Step 8).

When Joanne did this she concluded the following:

'While it is always possible for me to act or say something inappropriate at the formal dinner, I see now that I was overestimating the chances of me doing so. I did so because I have a more general tendency of awfulizing my behaviour when I am with people in formal social settings which I bring to my inferences at "A". Once I take the horror out of such things happening, I can put this into a more realistic perspective.'

I discuss coming back to 'A' in more detail later in this chapter.

Appendix 2 summarizes what Joanne did in each of the steps and Appendix 3 presents the steps that you need to follow in dealing with a specific example of your own anxiety and spaces for you to write down your own responses.

Dealing with anxiety: from the specific to the general

In the above section, I have shown you how to use the 'ABC' framework to assess and deal with a specific example of anxiety. You can use this with any specific example of anxiety.

In addition you can take a number of steps to deal with anxiety in a more general way.

IDENTIFY THREAT THEMES

When you have dealt with a number of specific examples of your anxiety, you may be able to identify one or more themes at 'A' that feature in your anxiety.

Here are some examples of such themes:

- ▶ the prospect of failing at important tasks
- ▶ the prospect of not being liked, loved or accepted
- ▶ not knowing that you are well or ill
- ▶ losing control of yourself
- ▶ acting inappropriately.

IDENTIFY CORE IRRATIONAL BELIEFS AND DEVELOP CORE RATIONAL BELIEFS

Core irrational beliefs are general irrational beliefs that are focused on a general theme such as those listed above. For example, let's assume that you tend to experience anxiety about the prospect of being rejected by significant others. Then, your core irrational belief might be: 'I must not be rejected by significant others and I am worthless if I am.' In which case your core rational belief will be something like: 'I don't want to be rejected by significant others, but that does not mean that this must not happen. If it does, I am fallible, not worthless.'

IDENTIFY ROUTINELY USED SAFETY-SEEKING MEASURES AND DEVELOP AND USE HEALTHY ALTERNATIVES

A major reason why people do not benefit from facing threat, even though we know that facing threat is the best way to deal with anxiety, is that they use a range of measures that are designed to keep us safe in the situation. The effect of using these safety-seeking measures is that you do not get to face the threat head on and therefore never really experience the benefit that *in vivo* exposure will give you.

Here is a list of commonly used safety-seeking measures used by people while being in situations that we find threatening.

Behavioural safety-seeking measures
Behavioural safety-seeking measures are those actions you undertake in a situation you find threatening in order to keep you safe from the threat. As I have said above, the consequence of using such measures is that you do not gain experience of actually facing and dealing with the threat.

Examples of such behavioural safety-seeking measures include:

▶ sitting at the end of a row so that you can get out of an auditorium easily
▶ sitting at the back of a room so that you are unnoticed
▶ sitting by a fan to stop yourself going red
▶ drinking alcohol to keep yourself from shaking
▶ using easy-to-pronounce words to stop yourself from stammering
▶ asking for reassurance to convince yourself that the threat is not real
▶ carrying out a variety of behavioural rituals all designed to show you that the threat won't occur (e.g. checking)
▶ carrying out a range of superstitious behaviours (e.g. having a lucky charm with you to ward off threat).

It is important that you do the opposite so that you can put yourself in a situation where you can deal with your threat. For example, instead of sitting by a fan to stop yourself from going red move away from the fan.

Cognitive safety-seeking measures
While behavioural safety-seeking measures involve you doing things to keep yourself safe in situations that you find threatening, cognitive safety-seeking measures are *internal* ways of achieving the same outcome. There are two types of such cognitive strategies:

1 where the content of your thinking is important
2 where the focus of your attention is important.

Here are some examples:

- ▶ seeking self-reassurance where you try to convince yourself that you are safe from the threat or that the consequences of facing the threat will be benign
- ▶ instead of this, accept the presence of the urge but do not engage with this form of thinking
- ▶ distracting yourself from the threat in some way (e.g. by focusing on some non-threatening aspect of the threatening situation)
- ▶ instead of doing this, focus back on the threat so you can deal with it.

While these safety-seeking measures largely interfere with you facing up to and dealing with the threat, there is some evidence that, if you use such a measure to get you into the situation and then relinquish it so that you focus on and respond to the threat as it is, then safety-seeking measures may have a beneficial effect.

IDENTIFY RECURRING SKEWED AND BIASED WAYS OF THINKING AND DEVELOP REALISTIC AND BALANCED ALTERNATIVES

In Chapter 2 I argued that when you hold irrational beliefs it affects the way you subsequently think. Thus, irrational beliefs tend to lead to subsequent thinking that is highly distorted and skewed to the negative and rational beliefs tend to lead to subsequent thinking that is realistic and balanced.

It is important that you identify recurring skewed and biased ways of thinking that stem from irrational beliefs and develop realistic and balanced ways of thinking that are based on rational beliefs. Table 9.2 described and illustrated the major thinking errors that stem from irrational beliefs and the realistic and balanced alternatives that are, in turn, based on rational beliefs.

Once you have identified the distorted thinking that stems from your irrational beliefs and the realistic and balanced thinking that is based on your rational beliefs, please bear in mind the following:

- ▶ Once you have challenged your irrational beliefs, it is important that you rehearse your realistic and balanced thinking for a time-limited period.
- ▶ Extensive focus on your realistic and balanced thinking is problematic. It may be that you are using this thinking to

reassure yourself that you are safe from threat. If so, this is a sign that your reassurance attempts are based on irrational thinking. In which case, you need to return to questioning your beliefs and in particular to showing yourself why your irrational beliefs are irrational and your rational beliefs are rational.

▶ Even when you have successfully challenged your irrational beliefs, you may still think in ways that are distorted and skewed to the negative. In Chapter 9 I referred to such thoughts as 'cognitive reverberations', which I explained by using the following analogy. Imagine that you are staring into an electric light and then you turn away from it. For a while you will have an after image of that light. The image reverberates on your retina. In the same way, even though you have challenged your irrational beliefs and are developing your rational beliefs, your subsequent distorted and skewed thinking may reverberate in your mind. You need to identify such thinking, recognize that it is a cognitive reverberation and do not engage with it. Accept, but do not necessarily like, its existence, but resolve to think and act in ways that are consistent with your rational beliefs.

▶ Finally, it is important that you understand that these recurring skewed and biased ways of thinking are effects of irrational thinking and not predictions of what will happen in the future. They do not predict reality; rather they are evidence of irrational thinking.

Insight

Recognizing that your highly distorted anxiety-based thinking stems from your irrational beliefs will help you to disengage from it and see that it has no predictive power.

LOOK AT YOUR PERCEIVED ABILITY TO DEAL WITH THREAT

As I explained earlier, one of the features of anxiety is that you hold the inference that you think that you cannot deal with threat. If you think that this is true, then you will not test it out and it will fan the flames of your feelings of anxiety. The best way of dealing with this idea is to subject it to empirical enquiry. This involves you recognizing that confidence develops from not being confident and that the more you act without 'unconfidence', the more you will develop confidence.

PRACTISE A PHILOSOPHY OF FACING THREAT

What I mean by a philosophy of facing threat is as follows. You recognize that you find certain things threatening. You prepare yourself to face these threats by developing and rehearsing rational beliefs. You plan to face the threats head on or, if a particular threat is overwhelming for you, at a given point in time, you resolve to face something with the same theme that is 'challenging but not overwhelming' for you. In actually facing the threats, you resolve not to use safety-seeking measures, but to use alternative healthy thinking and behavioural measures in their place. You do this until you no longer experience anxiety about the threats, but are duly concerned (or non-problematically anxious) instead.

DEVELOP A HEALTHY ATTITUDE TO ANXIETY ITSELF

In Chapter 14 I discussed a concept known as meta-emotional problems. This involves you focusing on your anxiety and then disturbing yourself about your anxious feelings. Quite often people feel anxious about the prospect of being anxious and this results in them avoiding situations that are only threatening to them because they may experience anxiety. Indeed, for many people the prospect of feeling anxious becomes their main threat.

The best way to deal with this is by assessing specific examples of this phenomenon using the 'Situational ABC' framework, questioning the resultant irrational and rational beliefs as discussed in Chapter 7 and then facing rather than avoiding situations where you are likely to feel anxious.

Insight

Sometimes your anxiety about your anxiety is your real anxiety problem.

The case of Bernice

Bernice experienced one episode of becoming anxious in a supermarket and had avoided going back ever since. In describing an example of her anxiety about anxiety, Bernice chose to describe a future scenario where she returns to the supermarket.

(Contd)

First, let's consider Bernice's 'Situational ABC' of her problem before presenting the 'Situational ABC' of her solution to the problem.

Situation	'If I go into a supermarket, I will become anxious'
'A'	Anxiety means I am beginning to lose control
'iB'	I must regain control of myself immediately, it would be terrible if I don't
'C' (emotional)	Increased anxiety (if I go to the supermarket alone)
'C' (behavioural)	Rushing out of supermarket if I am in there alone and have not taken a Diazepam Ensure whenever possible that I am accompanied by someone who can look after me if I have to go to the supermarket or, if I have to go alone, take a Diazepam first Avoid going to the supermarket and use the online shopping service instead
'C' (thinking)	If I don't gain control of myself immediately, I'll go crazy

Now let me present Bernice's 'Situational ABC' of her desired solution to her problem of anxiety about anxiety that she constructed after reading the material provided in this book. You should know that, as part of her solution, Bernice refrains from using the safety-seeking measures of taking a Diazepam and/or getting someone that she can rely on to accompany her.

Situation	'If I go into a supermarket, I will become anxious'
'A'	Anxiety means I am beginning to lose control
'rB'	I would like to regain control of myself immediately, but it is not necessary that I do so. It would be bad if I don't, but it would not be terrible

'C' (emotional)	*Concern*
'C' (behavioural)	*Staying in the supermarket*
'C' (thinking)	*If I don't gain control of myself immediately, in all probability what will happen is that I will continue to be anxious. It's unlikely that I'll go crazy*

Bernice then acted on her rational beliefs and went back to the supermarket several times without taking Diazepam and without having anyone accompany her. As a result of this, Bernice was able to deal effectively with her anxiety about anxiety. She also eventually developed a sense of confidence about dealing with feeling problematically anxious.

UNDERSTAND HOW UNCERTAINTY AND YOUR CORE BELIEFS AFFECT YOUR INFERENCES OF THREAT AT 'A' AND HOW TO EXAMINE 'A'

Remember that REBT encourages you to assume temporarily that the inferences that you make about the threat at 'A' in the 'ABC' framework are correct. We do this because we want you to focus on identifying your irrational beliefs at 'B', questioning them and developing a set of alternative rational beliefs. When you have done this, you are ready to come back to 'A' to examine it, for it may well be distorted.

Before you question your inferences at 'A', it is important to understand the mechanisms whereby you routinely make distorted inferences at 'A'. I explained this in Chapter 11, but will review it here. You will recall from Chapter 11 that there are two concepts you need to grasp in order to understand why and how you routinely make distorted inferences at 'A'. These are:

1 core irrational beliefs
2 uncertainty.

Core irrational beliefs
You will recall that, when you hold a specific irrational belief, then this irrational belief has specific referents. It concerns, for example, the specific behaviour (or absence of behaviour) of a specific person, in a specific location. This is why I liken the articulation of a specific irrational belief to a game of Cluedo (known as Clue in North America)

where, for example, one discovers that the murder was carried out by 'Colonel Mustard in the Dining Room with a Candelabra'. Thus, an example of a specific irrational belief is: 'When I give a presentation on Tuesday in the boardroom, the head of the company must like what I say and it would be terrible if she doesn't.'

By contrast, core irrational beliefs are general beliefs that relate to a specific theme but which span across situations and tend to involve a group or groups of people: Thus: 'Whenever I give presentations important people must like what I say and it would be terrible if they don't.'

Uncertainty

The theme of uncertainty is often found in specific episodes and general problems of anxiety that is problematic. When you are uncertain you do not know salient aspects of the situation that it is important to you to know. There are two different types of uncertainty:

1 uncertainty where you do not know what is going to happen, whether it is positive or negative
2 uncertainty where you do not know that a bad outcome will not happen.

In my experience, the second type of uncertainty is more prevalent in anxiety.

The formation of distorted inferences at 'A' when you relate the second type of uncertainty to your core irrational belief

In this section I will explain how your core irrational belief interacts with the second type of uncertainty to produce your distorted inference at 'A'. Let me detail this in a series of steps:

1 Let's assume that you hold the following core irrational belief: 'I must be approved by people whom I am attracted to.'
2 Let's further assume that you bring the second type of uncertainty to this core irrational belief. Here your revised core belief is: 'I must know that people to whom I am attracted approve of me.'
3 Imagine that you take this revised core irrational belief to a specific situation where there is a man, Simon, whom you find

attractive and you don't know whether or not he approves
of you.

4 Now because your core irrational belief is rigid, it leads in your
mind to two possibilities: either you know that Simon approves
of you or he doesn't. And since you cannot convince yourself
that he does approve of you, you then make the cognitive
conclusion that that he doesn't. In the episode in question,
then, the inference 'Simon does not approve of me' is your 'A'.

COMING BACK TO 'A'

In Chapter 10 I discussed how to deal with your distorted inferences
at 'A'. Basically, you deal with them after you have gotten yourself
into a rational frame of mind by questioning your irrational beliefs
and developing and strengthening your rational beliefs and then
you basically check your inference against the available evidence
(see Chapter 10).

However, a somewhat different way of dealing with distortions at
'A' follows on from what I have said about how we come to make
such distortions in the first place. This involves you doing the
following:

1 Focus on your distorted inference at 'A' – e.g. 'I will give a poor
presentation.'
2 Get yourself into a rational frame of mind by identifying
and questioning your irrational belief and developing and
strengthening your rational belief.
3 Come back to your inference and formulate your core irrational
belief by bringing together the theme of uncertainty with the
general irrational belief related to your 'A'. In this case the core
irrational belief is: 'I must know that I am going to give a good
presentation.' The cognitive conclusion from this core irrational
belief and which becomes your 'A' is: 'Since I cannot convince
myself that I will give a good presentation, then ... I will give a
poor presentation.' This conclusion is your 'A'.
4 See how your inference at 'A' is really constructed by your core
irrational belief interacting with uncertainty.

This material is presented in Figure 15.1.

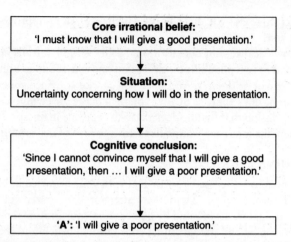

Core irrational belief:
'I must know that I will give a good presentation.'

↓

Situation:
Uncertainty concerning how I will do in the presentation.

↓

Cognitive conclusion:
'Since I cannot convince myself that I will give a good presentation, then ... I will give a poor presentation.'

↓

'A': 'I will give a poor presentation.'

Figure 15.1 How holding a core irrational belief influences the inferences we form at 'A' in anxiety.

5 Recognize that your 'A' has been formed by your core irrational belief and is probably not true.

6 Act as if the inference is incorrect and get on with your important life projects without engaging with the inference.

7 Then, if you need to, you can use the questions to check the validity of your inference at 'A' as I outlined in Chapter 10.

In the next chapter I will discuss how you can tackle depression.

THINGS TO REMEMBER

▶ You experience anxiety (and its healthy alternative, concern) when you face or think you face a threat to some important aspect of your personal domain.

▶ You feel anxious about a threat when you hold irrational beliefs about it and you feel concerned when you hold rational beliefs about the threat.

▶ In order to deal with your anxiety, it is important that you first replace your irrational belief with the alternative rational belief.

▶ Then take the remaining steps that I have discussed in the order that you think will help you the most.

▶ What is particularly curative in dealing with anxiety is acting in ways that are consistent with your rational beliefs. This means facing your threat sensibly while rehearsing your rational belief and without using any behavioural or cognitive safety-seeking measures.

▶ It is important that you develop a healthy attitude to anxiety. Otherwise you will feel anxious about the prospect of feeling anxious.

▶ You are likely to overestimate the existence of threat when you hold a core irrational belief that combines uncertainty with threat content and you bring this core belief to situations of ambiguity with respect to the existence of the threat.

▶ After you have begun to think rationally about the threat, you will be in a better frame of mind to view the threat realistically rather than exaggerate its nature and to reconsider your ability to cope with the threat.

16

....

Dealing with depression[1]

In this chapter you will learn:
- *the three routes into depression*
- *the important role that beliefs play in determining depression and its healthy alternative*
- *a step-by-step guide to assessing and dealing with specific instances of depression*
- *the importance of developing a healthy attitude to depression.*

When you experience depression (or its healthy alternative sadness):

▶ you have experienced a loss from your personal domain
▶ you have experienced a failure within your personal domain
▶ you or others have experienced an undeserved plight.

All this is true as long as your depression is psychologically based. As with anxiety, there are some medical conditions which cause depression. If you routinely cannot point to some kind of loss, failure or undeserved plight that you (or others) have experienced when you are depressed, it is again probably best to consult your GP/family doctor to rule out a medical cause before assuming that your depression is psychological in origin. I will make the assumption here that your depression is psychologically based.

[1]In this chapter I am talking about non-clinical depression. Clinical depression is characterized by a number of biological features such as insomnia, loss of appetite, loss of libido and suicidal ideation. If you think you may be clinically depressed, consult your GP/family doctor in the first instance.

Understanding depression by using the 'ABC' framework

As with anxiety and concern, you can use the 'ABC' framework to determine whether you feel depressed or sad.

The first 'ABC' framework outlines depression (Table 16.1).

Table 16.1 'ABC' formulation of depression.

'A'	▸ Loss ▸ Failure ▸ Undeserved plight befalling self or others
'B'	▸ You hold irrational beliefs about 'A'
'C' (emotional)	▸ Depression
'C' (behavioural) [Overt behaviour or action tendencies]	▸ You withdraw from others either straightaway or after an extended period of interpersonal clinginess ▸ You do not engage with mastery or pleasure-related activities ▸ You create an environment consistent with your depressed mood
'C' (thinking)	▸ You see the future as hopeless ▸ You see yourself as helpless ▸ You see others as being unsupportive or unavailable to you

The following 'ABC' framework outlines sadness (Table 16.2).

Table 16.2 'ABC' formulation of sadness.

'A'	▸ Loss ▸ Failure ▸ Undeserved plight befalling self or others
'B'	▸ You hold rational beliefs about 'A'
'C' (emotional)	▸ Sadness
'C' (behavioural) [Overt behaviour or action tendencies]	▸ You remain engaged with others in a non-clingy way ▸ You engage less with mastery or pleasure-related activities, but you remain engaged *(Contd)*

	▶ You create an environment consistent with your sad or non-problematically depressed mood
'C' (thinking)	▶ You see the future as difficult but you remain hopeful
	▶ You still see yourself as resourceful even though your resources have been challenged
	▶ You see significant others as being supportive and available to you

This again shows that you can distinguish between depression and sadness, not only by your beliefs (irrational in the former and rational in the latter) but also by considering what you do (or feel like doing) and how you think when you feel depression or sadness.

One of the main distinguishing features between depression and sadness is that in the former there is a general and pervasive shutting down of activity, an immediate or eventual withdrawal from the supportive and enriching features of life with a concomitant increase in skewed and distorted negative thinking. In sadness, by contrast, activity may be reduced, but there is still engagement with life and thinking is more balanced and realistic.

Insight

If you do not experience loss, failure or undeserved plight, then you will not be psychologically depressed (or sad). However, when you do experience one of these three things, you feel depressed because you hold irrational beliefs about it and you feel sad because you hold rational beliefs about it.

Three routes into depression

Psychologists have discovered that there are three major routes into depression: a sociotropic route, an autonomous route and a self- and/or other-pity route. Sociotropic depression occurs when you hold irrational beliefs about losses in your relationships with people. Autonomous depression occurs when you hold irrational beliefs when you experience losses or failures in your autonomous functioning in the world. Finally, depression based on self- and/or other-pity occurs when you and/or others experience some undeserved plight and you hold irrational beliefs about this plight. While a person may take more than one route, I will describe each one separately.

___

Sociotropic depression

This type of depression is based on your relationships with others. It comprises the following elements:

THE 'A' IN SOCIOTROPIC DEPRESSION

At 'A' in the 'ABC' framework you have (or think you have) experienced a disruption in your preferred way of relating to people. Thus:

- ▶ You may have been rejected.
- ▶ Someone who has looked after you stops doing so.
- ▶ You are separated from others.

THE 'B' IN SOCIOTROPIC DEPRESSION

At 'B' in the 'ABC' you hold an irrational belief about this 'A'. In this irrational belief the rigid belief is common, but in different types of sociotropic depression the extreme beliefs are different.

Sociotropic depression based on self-depreciation

Some people who experience sociotropic depression hold a rigid belief and a self-depreciation belief. For example, Peter was rejected by his girlfriend and experienced depression because his irrational belief was: 'My girlfriend absolutely should not have rejected me. I am unlovable because she did so.' In this type of depression, then, you base your self-esteem on certain conditions being present in your relationships with key people in your life and when these conditions are absent (or you think they are) then you depreciate yourself in some way.

Sociotropic depression based on discomfort intolerance

Other people who experience sociotropic depression hold a rigid belief and a discomfort intolerance belief. Such people believe that they need certain interpersonal conditions to be present in their lives and that they could not tolerate the absence of these conditions. For example, Harry formed relationships with women where they basically looked after him. When his current girlfriend left him he experienced depression. His irrational belief was: 'I must be looked after by a woman and if I'm not I can't bear the discomfort of having to do things for myself.' In this type of sociotropic depression the person often has a view of himself (in this case) as being helpless and lacking in self-care skills.

THE 'C' IN SOCIOTROPIC DEPRESSION

At 'C' in the 'ABC' sociotropic depression shows up mainly in your behaviour and subsequent thinking. Behaviourally, while you will eventually withdraw from people, initially you may seek support from them, but in a needy, childlike manner. This is particularly true when your sociotropic depression is based on discomfort intolerance and the sense that you are too weak to look after yourself. Since your stance in life is to be looked after rather than to help yourself, your clinging behaviour eventually becomes aversive to others who start off with good intentions to help you, but who then tend to withdraw from you, avoid you or even reject you. When this happens your depression deepens.

The content of your subsequent thinking is dominated by distorted views of the future in terms of your relationships. In sociotropic depression based on self-depreciation, your subsequent thinking reflects exaggerated consequences of being (in your own eyes) unlovable (e.g. you see yourself as being alone with nobody to love you). In sociotropic depression based on discomfort intolerance, your subsequent thinking reflects the idea that you are too weak to look after yourself and you see yourself as alone and uncared for with nobody to look after you.

Autonomous depression

This type of depression is based on your sense of autonomy. People who value autonomy within their personal domain are happiest when they are in control, when they are achieving important goals or are moving towards these goals without being hampered and when they are free to direct their own lives. However, when their sense of autonomy is diminished they are vulnerable to experiencing depression when they hold irrational beliefs when this is happening.

Autonomous depression comprises the following elements:

THE 'A' IN AUTONOMOUS DEPRESSION

At 'A' in the 'ABC' framework you have (or think you have) experienced a disruption in your autonomous functioning and your efforts to restore autonomy have failed. Thus:

- ▶ You may have failed at something important to you.
- ▶ You are in a position of being dependent on others.
- ▶ Your freedom has been curtailed with no chance of restoring it.

THE 'B' IN AUTONOMOUS DEPRESSION

At 'B' in the 'ABC' you hold an irrational belief about this 'A'. In this irrational belief the rigid belief is common, but in different types of autonomous depression the extreme beliefs are different.

Autonomous depression based on self-depreciation

Some people who experience autonomous depression hold a rigid belief and a self-depreciation belief. For example, Maureen failed to get promoted and as a result she was stuck in her existing job with no prospect of advancement. She experienced depression because her irrational belief was: 'I must continue to be promoted and I am a failure because I failed in this respect.' In this type of autonomous depression, you base your self-esteem on certain conditions related to the presence of autonomy and, when these conditions are absent (or you think they are), then you depreciate yourself in some way.

Autonomous depression based on discomfort intolerance

Other people who experience autonomous depression hold a rigid belief and a discomfort intolerance belief. Such people believe that they need certain autonomy-related conditions to be present in their lives and that they could not tolerate the absence of these conditions. For example, Jim broke both legs in a skiing accident and as a result he had to rely on his family to help him with everyday tasks that he had previously taken for granted. He became depressed because he held the following irrational belief: 'I must be able to look after myself and I can't bear relying on others.' As Jim said: 'I am not a weak person for relying on others; it's just that I can't bear the state of being helpless.'

THE 'C' IN AUTONOMOUS DEPRESSION

As with sociotropic depression, the distinctive features of autonomous depression at 'C' in the 'ABC' are evident mainly in your behaviour and subsequent thinking. Behaviourally, you will initially try to deny how you feel to others and carry on as normal. When this fails, you will remove yourself from others partly because of the general tendency to withdraw into yourself that occurs in all forms of depression and partly because you don't want them to see you in a non-coping state.

The content of your subsequent thinking is dominated by distorted views of the future in terms of autonomy. In autonomous depression based on self-depreciation, your subsequent thinking reflects the idea that others see you as weak and worthless for lacking control over your own life. In autonomous depression based on discomfort intolerance, your subsequent thinking exaggerates your lack of autonomy and you see yourself as having far less autonomy than you actually have. You also think that others pity you for your lack of autonomy. Being pitied is a highly aversive interpersonal reaction for people with a need for autonomy.

Depression based on self-pity or other-pity

This type of depression has to do with your attitude to an undeserved plight that has befallen you or others. It is comprised of the following elements:

THE 'A' IN PITY-RELATED DEPRESSION

At 'A' in the 'ABC' framework an undeserved plight has (or you think that it has) happened to you or to others. Here are some examples:

▶ You may have been made redundant by a company after working very hard for it for many years.
▶ A major catastrophe happens to people who are already struggling with their lives.

THE 'B' IN PITY-BASED DEPRESSION

At 'B' in the 'ABC' you hold an irrational belief about this 'A'. In both self-pity depression and other-pity depression, there are the following irrational beliefs:

▶ a rigid belief
▶ an awfulizing belief
▶ a discomfort intolerance belief
▶ a life-depreciation belief.

Let me illustrate this.

Self-pity depression

Frank was made redundant after working very hard for his company for many years. He experienced self-pity based depression because he held the following irrational beliefs:

▶ *Rigid belief*: 'I absolutely should not have been made redundant after all I have done for the company.'

- *Awfulizing belief*: 'It's terrible that my company made me redundant after all I did for them.'
- *Discomfort intolerance belief*: 'I can't stand this undeserved plight.'
- *Life-depreciation*: 'The world is a rotten place for allowing this to happen to me.'

Other-pity depression

Marlene was a volunteer in Haiti working among the poor. When the earthquake happened, the people she was working with experienced devastation to their already meagre living conditions. Marlene experienced other-pity depression because she held the following beliefs:

- *Rigid belief*: 'This additional catastrophe absolutely should not have happened to these people who do not deserve it.'
- *Awfulizing belief*: 'It's terrible that this has happened to them.'
- *Discomfort intolerance belief*: 'I can't stand it that this undeserved plight has happened to them.'
- *Life-depreciation*: 'The world is a rotten place for allowing this to happen to them.'

THE 'C' IN PITY-BASED DEPRESSION

At 'C' in the 'ABC' the distinctive features of self-pity and other-pity depression show up mainly in your behaviour and subsequent thinking. Behaviourally, while you will eventually withdraw from people, initially you will complain about how unfairly life has treated you and/or others. While you may receive a sympathetic response at the outset, your continued complaining will lead others to move away from you or to become angry with you. At that point you will withdraw into yourself.

The content of your subsequent thinking is dominated by distorted views of the world and the future. Here, you tend to see the world as being dominated by undeserved plight rather than as a complex mixture of the good, the bad and the neutral. Additionally you tend to view the future as filled with undeserved plight. In addition you tend to see yourself as a poor person who is being unfairly treated and others as poor people again who are being poorly treated.

Insight

The key to feeling sad rather than depressed about an event is to hold rational beliefs about the loss / failure / undeserved plight. But these beliefs will only take hold when you act and think in ways that are consistent with them.

Dealing with depression: overview

The above analysis suggests that to deal with your depression you need to do the following:

RAISE YOUR LEVEL OF ACTIVITY

Focusing on your irrational beliefs while you are inactive and depressed is like trying to walk up a straight with heavy weights strapped around your ankles. It is best not to try it. If you think you can't be more active, put that to the test. Would you move if a smoke alarm went off? Probably. So you can do it! Take some active steps even though you don't feel like it. Once you have become a bit more active, you will be likely to extend this. Taking things bit by bit with respect to being more active will soon pay off if you let it.

REPLACE YOUR IRRATIONAL BELIEFS

Once you are more active, you are in a better position to replace your irrational belief with its rational alternative in the ways that I have outlined in Chapter 7.

TALK ABOUT YOUR FEELINGS WITH SUPPORTIVE OTHERS

Once you have got yourself into a more rational frame of mind, allow yourself to feel sad and to talk about your feelings with supportive others who will allow you to experience and talk about your sadness in your own way. Focusing on your loss, failure or undeserved plight in this way will allow you to digest and work through the salient issues so that you can process it, integrate it and move on with your life at your own pace and in your own way.

Having respect for your own way of dealing with loss etc. is very important. While there are models of the process of mourning loss, for example, these are normative models (i.e. based on the experience of many) and, as far as you can, do not attempt to modify your own idiosyncratic experience so that it fits the norm.

> **Insight**
> Talking to supportive others when you are depressed will help you to stay connected to others and counter your strong tendency to withdraw into yourself.

RENEW YOUR COMMITMENT TO YOUR LIFE'S GOALS OR DEVELOP AND PURSUE NEW GOALS

Once you have processed your loss and integrated it into your way of viewing the world, you can then renew your commitment to your life's goals and re-involve yourself in mastery and pleasure-related activities. However, your depressive episode may have encouraged you to rethink your priorities and set new goals. If this is the case, commit yourself to pursuing these new goals.

Dealing with depression: a specific example

Mike tends to experience self-depreciation autonomous depression when he fails at important tasks. His latest episode of depression occurred when a bid that he led for an external contract was unsuccessful. I will soon show you how Mike used the 'Situational ABC' framework to assess his problem. Note that I am proceeding on the assumption that Mike was sufficiently active to carry out an 'ABC' assessment of the specific episode of depression.

GET YOURSELF ACTIVE BEFORE USING THE 'SITUATIONAL ABC' FRAMEWORK

However, if Mike was not sufficiently active to use the 'Situational ABC' framework, he would need to become so before filling in the 'Situational ABC' form (see Appendix 1). Becoming more active involves the following:

▶ Identify actions that will help you achieve your important goals. These goals may be immediate ones, such as consistently getting up in the morning, making coffee, and leaving the house, or longer-term ones, such as looking for a new job.
▶ Break these activities into manageable chunks.
▶ Take action no matter what you are thinking and feeling. This is particularly important. People who are depressed usually let their thinking and feeling influence what they are going to do. It is important that you don't do this. Instead, the message is: Feel what you feel and think what you think but act according to your goals.

USING THE 'SITUATIONAL ABC' FRAMEWORK TO ASSESS A SPECIFIC EXAMPLE OF DEPRESSION

This is how Mike used the 'Situational ABC' framework to assess this example of his autonomous depression. Again, I suggest that you follow the same schema in assessing a specific example of your own depression.

Step 1: Describe the situation
Mike described the situation in which he became depressed as follows:

> 'The bid for the external contract that I headed up was not successful.'

Step 2: Identify the unhealthy negative emotion in the situation (emotional 'C')
Mike identified his unhealthy negative emotion as follows:

> 'Depression'

Step 3: How I act and think when I feel depressed (behavioural 'C' and thinking 'C')
Mike identified the behavioural 'C' and thinking 'C' that accompanied his depression. In this way he knew that he felt depressed rather than sad:

> 'I seriously thought about handing in my resignation and I went out to get very drunk.'

Step 4: What I am most depressed about in the situation at 'A'
Mike identified his 'A' as follows:

> 'I am most depressed about failing to do a good job on the bid.'

Please note that, according to standard REBT practice, Mike assumed temporarily that he did fail to do a good job on the bid. He will have a chance to examine this inference later once he has got himself into a rational frame of mind.

Step 5: What is my rigid belief and main extreme belief at 'B' that accounts for my depression
Mike identified his two irrational beliefs as follows:

> 'I absolutely should have done a good job and the fact that I didn't proves that I am a failure.'

In Steps 6 and 7 Mike outlines what would constitute a healthier way of dealing with the failure. Note again that he formulates alternative rational beliefs and specifies how these would lead to a very different set of consequences for him.

Step 6: Formulating alternative rational beliefs
It is important that Mike formulates rational alternatives to his irrational beliefs before he begins to question them. Otherwise he may wish to give up his irrational beliefs, but have nothing to take their place.

Mike formulated the following rational beliefs as alternatives to his rigid belief and self-depreciation belief:

> *'I wish I had done a good job, but I didn't have to do one. I am not a failure, I am a fallible human being who is capable of doing well and poorly.'*

Step 7: Specifying goals (the healthy alternatives to depression and the behaviour and thinking that accompany it)
As you will recall, the purpose of using REBT with your problems is to respond to adversities in a healthy manner with respect to your feelings and the behaviour and thinking that accompany them. These are the goals that you are aiming for. They are also the consequences of holding the rational beliefs that you formulated in Step 6. It follows that you need to be clear with yourself what these goals are.

Mike specified his emotional, behavioural and thinking goals as follows:

> *'I am aiming to feel sad, but not depressed, about not doing a good job on the bid and to think that I need to review my performance rather than resign. Instead of going out to get drunk, I can get feedback from my team and learn from what they have to say.'*

Step 8: Questioning beliefs
As discussed in Chapter 7, the purpose of questioning beliefs is for you to understand the irrationality of irrational beliefs and the rationality of your rational beliefs. This provides the platform for the behaviour and the thinking that you need to subsequently engage in to help you address your problematic depression.

Mike wrote down his irrational beliefs and rational beliefs side by side and using the arguments discussed in Chapter 7 showed himself that his rational beliefs were true, logical and helpful, and that his irrational beliefs were false, illogical and unhelpful.

> *'I value doing well and wanted to do well on the bid, but that does not mean that I had to do well on it. If I had to do well,*

then I would have had to have done well. It is clear that there is no law of the universe that decrees that I have to do well. If there was, I could not go against it. I could literally not fail. Also, I am not a failure for failing to do well. My identity cannot be defined by my performance on the bid. I can prove that I am a fallible human being who is capable of doing well and poorly. If I were a failure then all I could do was fail and that is not the case.'

Step 9: Taking action and thinking in ways that are consistent with your rational beliefs

Step 9 is very important. If you don't act and think in ways that are consistent with your developing rational beliefs, then your conviction in these beliefs will remain intellectual and they have little impact on your feelings. If you act and think in ways that are consistent with these rational beliefs, and refrain from acting and thinking in ways that are consistent with your irrational beliefs, then you will strengthen your conviction in your rational beliefs and they will have a constructive impact on your emotions at 'C'.

> *'Since it was important to me that I did well on the bid, I used my rational desire to review what had happened (subsequent thinking) instead of thinking about resigning, and to ask my team for feedback (behaviour) instead of getting drunk.'*

Step 10: Coming back to 'A'

In REBT, we recommend that you initially assume that 'A' is true temporarily (see Step 4) and that the best time to come back to 'A' to re-evaluate it is when you have gotten yourself into a rational frame of mind (see Step 8).

When Mike did this he concluded the following:

> *'While it is true that we did not win the bid, when I think about my performance objectively and from the feedback I got from my team, I can see now that, while I made a few minor mistakes, I basically did do a good job on the bid. The general consensus among my team is that the company that won the bid did so because they had more money to spend on their bid than we did on ours.'*

Appendix 4 summarizes what Mike did in each of the steps and Appendix 5 presents the steps that you need to follow in dealing with a specific example of your own depression and spaces for you to write down your own responses.

Dealing with depression: from the specific to the general

In the above section I have shown you how to use the 'Situational ABC' framework to assess and deal with a specific example of depression. You can use this with any specific example of depression.

In addition, you can take a number of steps to deal with depression in a more general way.

IDENTIFY 'DEPRESSIVE' THEMES

When you have dealt with a number of specific examples of your depression, you may be able to identify one or more themes at 'A' that feature in your depression.

Here are some examples of such themes grouped according to the three types of depression discussed earlier in the chapter: sociotropic, autonomous and pity-based depression. Please note that, in these themes, I am talking about recurring events that either do reflect reality or that you think reflect reality. The latter are known as inferential themes.

Themes in sociotropic depression

- ▶ being disliked
- ▶ not being loved
- ▶ being rejected
- ▶ not having others to rely on
- ▶ being cut off from people
- ▶ being or 'feeling' emotionally alone
- ▶ not being cared for by others

Themes in autonomous depression

- ▶ failing at important tasks
- ▶ not being in as much control of your life as you prefer
- ▶ having your autonomy and freedom curtailed
- ▶ experiencing weakness
- ▶ displaying weakness
- ▶ being stuck
- ▶ having to rely on others
- ▶ being dependent on others

Themes in pity-based depression

▶ You are the undeserved victim of plight.
▶ Others are the undeserved victim of plight.

IDENTIFY CORE IRRATIONAL BELIEFS AND DEVELOP CORE RATIONAL BELIEFS

Core irrational beliefs that render a person vulnerable to depression are general irrational beliefs that are focused on a general theme such as those listed above. For example, let's assume that you tend to experience depression about undeserved plight. Then your core irrational belief might be: 'I must not experience undeserved plight and the world is a rotten place for letting this happen to me.' In which case your core rational belief will be something like: 'I would much prefer it if I do not experience undeserved plight but, sadly and regretfully, I am not immune from experiencing this and nor do I have to be so immune. The world is not a rotten place. It is a complex mixture of the fair and unfair.'

IDENTIFY RECURRING SKEWED AND BIASED WAYS OF THINKING AND DEVELOP REALISTIC AND BALANCED ALTERNATIVES

In Chapter 2 of this book I argued that when you hold irrational beliefs it affects the way you subsequently think. Thus, irrational beliefs tend to lead to subsequent thinking that is highly distorted and skewed to the negative and rational beliefs tend to lead to subsequent thinking that is realistic and balanced.

In depression, your core irrational beliefs tend to lead to subsequent thinking that is marked by negative views about yourself, others and the world. In particular you tend to think that you are helpless to deal with the adversities at 'A' and that as you look at the future you experience a sense of hopelessness about it.

As I argued in Chapter 9, it is important that you both identify recurring skewed and biased ways of thinking that stem from irrational beliefs and develop realistic and balanced ways of thinking that are based on rational beliefs (see Table 9.2).

Thus, it is important that:

▶ You see yourself, others and the world as a complex mixture of good, bad and neutral features.

- ▶ You recognize that while you may struggle you have resources to help yourself and that you are not helpless.
- ▶ You see the future as likely to involve good, bad and neutral things happening.

Initially, you will probably find such realistic and balanced views theoretically correct but emotionally unconvincing. This is to be expected and is a natural part of the change process. However, if you hold these thoughts in place as you act in ways that are consistent with your rational beliefs, then you will find yourself 'feeling' them as well as just thinking them.

The same caveats that I discussed in Chapter 9 about dealing with distorted subsequent thinking apply here, namely:

- ▶ Once you have challenged your irrational beliefs, rehearse your realistic and balanced thinking for a time-limited period only. Don't try and convince yourself of them. If you do, you will begin to ruminate on them and this is a sure way of maintaining rather than effectively dealing with your depression. When you rehearse your realistic and balanced thinking this will involve you responding to your distorted and skewed thinking. When you do this you are engaging with such distorted thinking. Engaging with these thoughts productively is akin to getting fit. You do so bit by bit and not all at once. That is why I recommend that you rehearse your realistic and balanced thinking for a time-limited period. If you try to get fit in one training session, you will be doomed to failure. Similarly if you try to thoroughly convince yourself that your realistic and balanced thinking is true and productive then you will be doomed to failure here as well.
- ▶ Accept, then, that your distorted and skewed subsequent thinking may reverberate for a while. The best way to deal with this is to accept, but not like, this fact and act towards your healthy goals even though these distorted thoughts are in your mind. Take action, then, without engaging with these thoughts. Don't worry, though, if you find yourself engaging with these thoughts. Just accept that you are and then disengage from them while taking goal-directed action with these thoughts in your mind.
- ▶ Finally, as I pointed out in Chapter 9, it is important that you understand that these recurring skewed and biased ways of

thinking are effects of irrational thinking and not predictions of what will happen in the future.

ACT IN WAYS THAT ARE CONSISTENT WITH YOUR CORE RATIONAL BELIEFS AND INCONSISTENT WITH YOUR CORE IRRATIONAL BELIEFS

In order for you to change your core irrational beliefs and develop your conviction in your core rational beliefs, it is important that you act in ways that are consistent with the latter and inconsistent with the former. Such behavioural change needs to be:

▶ maintained over time
▶ based on rehearsal of your core rational beliefs and specific variants of these core beliefs
▶ combined with realistic and balanced subsequent thinking.

Here is an example. Derek developed the following core rational belief:

'I want women to whom I am attracted to fancy me, but they do not have to do so. If they don't fancy me, I am not worthless; I can accept myself as a fallible human being capable of being fancied and not fancied by these women.'

Derek kept approaching women to whom he was attracted and rehearsed this core rational belief (and its specific variants) as he did so. He also reminded himself that, if attractive women don't fancy him, it is unlikely that they will scorn him, but if this happens it will be a rare occurrence. It is more likely that they will think that he is a nice guy but not boyfriend material. Taking this tack, Derek was rejected by several women, which he found disappointing but not depressing. He eventually found an attractive woman who did fancy him.

PRACTISE A PHILOSOPHY OF SELF-COMPASSION (BASED ON FLEXIBLE ENGAGEMENT TOGETHER WITH SUITABLE PROCESSING TIME)

What I mean by a philosophy of self-compassion based on flexible engagement together with suitable processing time is as follows.

If you are vulnerable to depression, then you will tend to disengage from mastery and pleasure-related tasks and withdraw into yourself. If you have experienced a loss, a failure or an undesired plight, it would be unrealistic to expect you to maintain a full engagement with such activities, but neither do you have to disengage from them completely other than for a short period. Your rational beliefs will allow you to disengage partly from such tasks so that you can process what has happened to you in your own way and in your own time. You can do this processing on your own, but seeking support from people who will allow you to talk things through in your own way is also helpful.

Think of this philosophy as one where you show yourself compassion. Would you expect someone you care for who has experienced a significant loss, for example, to remain fully engaged with life? Probably not. Would you recommend that they completely disengage from life for a long period? Again, probably not. You would probably recommend that they take some time out to recover and look after themselves and stay somewhat engaged with people and activities that are important to them and to gradually return to the fold, as it were, as their positive mood returned. In a word, you would show them compassion. Showing yourself compassion is an important way out of your depression as my friend and colleague Professor Paul Gilbert has shown in his book *The Compassionate Mind* (Constable, 2009).

DEVELOP A HEALTHY ATTITUDE TO DEPRESSION

In Chapter 14 I discussed a concept known as meta-emotional problems. With respect to depression, this involves you focusing on your depression then disturbing yourself about your depressed feelings, your depressed thinking or your depressed behaviour. Quite often people feel depressed about being depressed, which results in them deepening their depression. This is particularly the case with those people whose original depression is autonomous in nature (see above).

Again, the best way to deal with this is by assessing specific examples of this phenomenon using the 'Situational ABC' framework, questioning the resultant irrational and rational beliefs as discussed in Chapter 7.

In the case that follows, George experienced depression for the first time in his life when he lost his job as a marketing consultant. Being autonomous in personality structure he quickly depressed himself about his depression.

Here is George's 'Situational ABC' of his problem, before we present the 'Situational ABC' of his solution to the problem.

Situation	*I got depressed when I lost my job*
'A'	*Getting depressed over losing my job is pathetic*
'iB'	*I must not react so pathetically and I am a weak pathetic person because I did so*
'C' (emotional)	*Increased depression*
'C' (behavioural)	*Going to bed to sleep as much as I can*
'C' (thinking)	*If I can't handle losing my job then my future is completely bleak*

Now let me present George's 'Situational ABC' of his desired solution to his problem of depression about depression that he formulated after reading the material provided in this book.

Situation	*I got depressed when I lost my job*
'A'	*Getting depressed over losing my job is pathetic*
'iB'	*I would like not to react so pathetically, but I don't have to be immune from reacting in this way. I am not a weak pathetic person because I did so. Rather, I am a fallible human being who has strengths and weaknesses and at present feeling depressed is my Achilles heel*
'C' (emotional)	*Disappointment about being depressed*
'C' (behavioural)	*Getting up early and becoming more active*
'C' (thinking)	*Just because I can't handle losing my job at present does not mean that my future is completely bleak. My future is in my hands and I am going to concentrate on dealing with my depression before contemplating my future*
Coming back to 'A'	*Getting depressed is not pathetic. It is a consequence of holding a rigid belief*

George then acted on his rational beliefs and began to organize his day around becoming more active rather than withdrawing into himself. As he became more active, he then dealt with his original depression which was based on the idea that he must never lose a job and that he was useless because he did. As he dealt with that irrational belief, he began to organize himself to apply for new jobs. After three months he found a new job. He later said that the main advantage of being depressed and depressed about being depressed was that it taught him how rigid he was and how lacking in self-compassion. He used this to develop a more flexible and compassionate attitude towards himself.

Insight

When you disturb yourself about being depressed, you experience double depression. It is thus so important that you develop rational beliefs about being depressed.

UNDERSTAND HOW UNCERTAINTY AND YOUR CORE BELIEFS AFFECT YOUR INFERENCES AT 'A' WHEN YOU ARE DEPRESSED AND HOW TO EXAMINE 'A'

As I have mentioned several times in this book, REBT encourages you to assume temporarily that the inferences that you make of loss, failure or undeserved plight at 'A' in the 'ABC' framework are correct. We do this because we want you to focus on identifying your irrational beliefs at 'B' so that you can question them and develop a set of alternative rational beliefs. If you examine 'A' first and correct any distortions that you find there, then you are less motivated to go on to identify, question and change your irrational beliefs at 'B'. When you have focused on 'B' and developed your new set of rational beliefs, then you are ready to come back to 'A' to examine it, for, as I have noted, it may well be distorted.

If you discover that you routinely make the same distortions at 'A', it is important to understand the process whereby this happens. As I discussed in the corresponding section in the previous chapter, when you face uncertainty where you do not know that a loss, a failure or some undeserved plight has not happened, you bring your core irrational beliefs to this sense of uncertainty. You will recall that core irrational beliefs are general beliefs that relate to a specific theme (such as loss, failure and undeserved plight), but span across situations and tend to involve a group or groups of people. Thus: 'I must do well at important tasks and I am a failure if I don't.'

Here is how your core irrational belief interacts with uncertainty to produce your distorted inference at 'A':

▶ You hold the following core irrational belief: 'I must do well at important tasks and I am a failure if I don't.'
▶ You bring uncertainty (where you don't know that an adversity has not happened) to this core irrational belief. Here your revised core belief is: 'I must know that I have done well at important tasks.'

Imagine that you take this revised core irrational belief to a specific situation where you have written an exam but you do not know that you have done well on the exam.

Now because your core irrational belief is rigid, it leads in your mind to two possibilities: either you know that you have done well on the exam or you have done poorly on it. Since you cannot convince yourself that you have done well, you conclude that you have done poorly. In the episode in question, then, the inference 'I have done poorly on the exam' is your 'A'.

COMING BACK TO 'A'

As you will recall, in Chapter 10 I discussed how to deal with your distorted inferences at 'A'. You first get yourself into a rational frame of mind by questioning your irrational beliefs and developing and strengthening your rational beliefs and then you basically check your inference against the available evidence (see Chapter 10).

However, as I pointed out in the previous chapter, a different way of dealing with distortions at 'A' follows on from what I have said about how we come to make such distortions in the first place.

This involves you doing the following:

1 Focus on your distorted inference at 'A'. For example, 'My friends are disgusted with me for getting depressed'.
2 Get yourself into a rational frame of mind by identifying and questioning your irrational belief and developing and strengthening your rational belief.
3 Come back to your inference and formulate your core irrational belief by bringing together the theme of uncertainty with the

general irrational belief related to your 'A'. In this case the core irrational belief is: 'I must know that my friends will approve of me, no matter what'. The cognitive conclusion from this core irrational belief and which becomes your 'A' is: 'Since I cannot convince myself that my friends will approve of me no matter what then ... My friends will be disgusted with me for getting depressed'. This latter conclusion is your 'A'.

4 See how your inference at 'A' is really constructed by your core irrational belief interacting with uncertainty.

This material is presented in Figure 16.1.

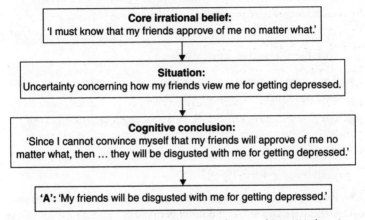

Figure 16.1 How holding a core irrational belief influences the inferences we form at 'A' in depression.

5 Recognize that your 'A' has been formed by your core irrational belief and is probably not true.

6 Act as if the inference is incorrect and get on with your important life projects without engaging with the inference.

7 Then, if you need to, you can use the questions to check the validity of your inference at 'A', as I outlined in Chapter 10.

THINGS TO REMEMBER

▶ You experience depression (and its healthy alternative, sadness) when you have experienced or think you have experienced a loss/failure or when you or others have experienced an undeserved plight.

▶ You feel depressed about these things when you hold irrational beliefs about them and you feel sad when you hold rational beliefs about them.

▶ In order to deal with your depression, you first need to be sufficiently active to do so.

▶ Then it is important that you first replace your irrational belief with the alternative rational belief.

▶ Then take the remaining steps that I have discussed in the order that you think will help you the most.

▶ What is particularly curative in dealing with depression is again acting in ways that are consistent with your rational beliefs. This means facing the loss, failure or undeserved plight, while thinking rationally about them.

▶ It is important that you develop a healthy attitude to depression. Otherwise you will feel doubly depressed.

▶ You are likely to overestimate the existence of loss, failure or undeserved plight when you hold a core irrational belief that combines uncertainty with such elements and you bring this core belief to situations of ambiguity with respect to the existence of the relevant element.

▶ After you have begun to think rationally about the loss / failure / undeserved plight, you will be in a better frame of mind to view it realistically rather than be hopeless and/or helpless in the face of it.

▶ Developing a philosophy of self-compassion when tackling depression will help prevent its reoccurrence.

We have now reached the end of the book. I do hope that you have found it instructive and valuable. I would appreciate receiving any feedback c/o the publisher.

Taking it further

Relevant websites

www.windydryden.com
This is my own professional website.

www.arebt.org
This is the website for the Association for Rational Emotive Behaviour Therapy, the professional body for REBT therapists in the UK.

www.rebt.org
This is the website for the Albert Ellis Institute, the premier centre for the promotion of REBT internationally.

www.babcp.com
This is the website for the British Association for Behavioural and Cognitive Psychotherapies, the lead organization for Cognitive Behaviour Therapy in the UK.

References and further reading

Beck, A.T. (1976). *Cognitive Therapy and the Emotional Disorders* (New York: International Universities Press).

Burns, D.D. (1980). *Feeling Good: The New Mood Therapy* (New York: William Morrow).

Burns, D.D. (1989). *The Feeling Good Handbook* (New York: William Morrow).

Dryden, W. (1994). *Ten Steps to Positive Living* (London: Sheldon Press).

Dryden, W. (2000). *Overcoming Anxiety* (London: Sheldon).

Dryden, W. (2001). *Reason to Change: A Rational Emotive Behaviour Therapy (REBT) Workbook* (Hove, East Sussex: Brunner-Routledge).

Dryden, W. (2009). *Understanding Emotional Problems: The REBT Perspective* (Hove, East Sussex: Routledge).

Dryden, W. & Opie, S. (2003). *Overcoming Depression* (London: Sheldon).

Ellis, A. (1984). *How to Maintain and Enhance your Rational-Emotive Therapy Gains* (New York: Albert Ellis Institute).

Ellis, A. (1994). *Reason and Emotion in Psychotherapy,* revised and updated edition (New York: Birch Lane Press).

Ellis, A. (2002). *Overcoming Resistance: A Rational-Emotive Behavior Therapy Integrated Approach,* second edition (New York: Springer).

Gilbert, P. (2009). *The Compassionate Mind: A New Approach to Life's Challenges* (London: Constable).

Maslow, A. (1968). *Toward a Psychology of Being* (New York: Van Nostrand Reinhold).

Neenan, M. (2009). *Developing Resilience: A Cognitive-Behavioral Approach* (Hove: Routledge).

Neenan, M. & Dryden, W. (2002). *Life Coaching: A Cognitive-Behavioural Approach* (Hove: Brunner-Routledge).

Wilding, C. & Palmer, S. (2010). *Beat Low Self-esteem with CBT* (London: Hodder Education).

Willson, R. & Branch, R. (2006). *Cognitive Behavioural Therapy for Dummies* (Chichester: John Wiley & Sons).

Appendix 1: 'Situational ABC' blank form with instructions

'SITUATION' =

'A' =

'iB' (irrational belief) =   **'rB' (rational belief) =**

'C' (emotional consequence) =   **'C' (emotional goal) =**

'C' (behavioural consequence) =   **'C' (behavioural goal) =**

'C' (thinking consequence) =   **'C' (thinking goal) =**

1 Write down a brief, objective description of the 'situation' you were in.
2 Identify your 'C' – your major disturbed emotion, your dysfunctional behaviour and, if relevant, your distorted subsequent thinking.

3 Identify your 'A' – this is what you were most disturbed about in the situation (Steps 2 and 3 are interchangeable).

4 Set emotional, behavioural and thinking goals.

5 Identify your irrational beliefs ('iBs') i.e. rigid belief plus one of the following extreme beliefs: awfulizing belief, discomfort intolerance belief or deprecation belief (self, others or life).

6 Identify the alternative rational beliefs ('rBs') that will enable you to achieve your goals i.e. flexible belief plus one of the following non-extreme beliefs: non-awfulizing belief, discomfort tolerance or acceptance belief (self, others or life).

Appendix 2: How Joanne dealt with a specific example of her anxiety

Step 1: Describe the situation	*'Sitting at the dinner table at the firm's annual dinner.'*
Step 2: Identify the unhealthy negative emotion in the situation (emotional 'C')	*Anxiety*
Step 3: How I act and think when I feel anxious (behavioural 'C' and thinking 'C')	*'When I feel anxious, I anticipate thinking that if I do anything inappropriate then everyone will notice and judge me negatively. I will therefore say nothing, but wish that I could escape.'*
Step 4: What I am most anxious about in the situation ('A')	*'I am most anxious about saying or doing something inappropriate at the formal dinner.'*
Step 5: What is my rigid belief and main extreme belief at 'B' that accounts for my anxiety	*'I must not say or do anything inappropriate and it would be terrible if I do.'*
Step 6: Formulating alternative rational beliefs	*'I would prefer it if I do not say or do anything inappropriate, but it doesn't follow that I must not do so. If I do it would be bad, but not terrible.'*
Step 7: Specifying goals (the healthy alternatives to anxiety and the behaviour and thinking that accompany it)	*'I am aiming to feel concerned, but not anxious, about saying or doing anything inappropriate in the situation and to think that if I do then some people might*

(Contd)

	notice and judge me, but most probably won't. I am also aiming to speak up and enjoy myself as best I can.'
Step 8: Questioning beliefs	*'I can see that it is always possible for me to say something inappropriate at the dinner and for me to demand that I must not do so does not remove the possibility. Indeed, this demand may even increase the possibility that I may say something inappropriate because it leads to me being very anxious which in turn interferes with me being able to concentrate on the conversations. However, it is true that I would prefer it if I did not say something inappropriate, and it is also true that I don't have to be immune from doing so. Also, while it would be unfortunate if I said something inappropriate, it is hardly awful if I do so. There are far worse things that could happen to people so I am going to view it within a much wider framework.'*
Step 9: Identifying behavioural and cognitive safety-seeking measures and their healthy alternatives	1 *Behavioural safety-seeking measures and their healthy alternatives (in brackets)* ▷ *Agreeing with people (Speaking my mind)* ▷ *Going to the toilet when feeling uncomfortable (Staying at the table when feeling uncomfortable)*

	2 *Cognitive safety-seeking measures and their healthy alternatives (in brackets)*
	▷ *Distracting myself when feeling uncomfortable (Acknowledging and accepting my discomfort)*
	▷ *Rehearsing everything that I plan to say so that I don't sound stupid (Saying what I want to say without mentally rehearsing it first)*
Step 10: Facing the specific threat in imagination while mentally rehearsing rational beliefs and acting and thinking accordingly	*'I focused on speaking up at the dinner and on the possibility that I might say something inappropriate until I experienced feelings of problematic anxiety. I then used this as a cue to rehearse my rational belief (i.e. "I would prefer it if I do not say or do anything inappropriate, but it doesn't follow that I must not do so. If I do it would be bad, but not terrible"). I saw myself feeling concerned, but not anxious, which helped me to speak up and I reminded myself that, if I did say something inappropriate, some people would notice and judge me negatively, but most probably wouldn't.'*
Step 11: Facing the specific threat in reality while mentally rehearsing	*'I went to the dinner and faced my fear by speaking up at the dinner table, disagreeing*

(Contd)

rational beliefs and acting and thinking accordingly	*several times with people who expressed views contrary to my own. While doing this, I rehearsed my rational belief that while I would prefer not to say anything inappropriate, sadly I am not immune from doing so nor do I have to be immune. If I did say anything inappropriate, that would be nasty, but it would not be the end of the universe. I noticed when I was tempted to use safety-seeking behaviour and thinking, but used my healthy behavioural and thinking alternatives instead.* *Finally, I reminded myself that even if I did act inappropriately, most others would probably not notice my behaviour. This helped me to focus on engaging in conversation with people rather than on what they might be thinking about me.'*
Step 12: Coming back to 'A'	*'While it is always possible for me to act or say something inappropriate at the formal dinner, I see now that I was overestimating the chances of me doing so. I did so because I have a more general tendency of awfulizing my behaviour when I am with people in formal social settings. Once I take the horror out of such things happening, I can put this into a more realistic perspective.'*

Appendix 3: 12 steps in dealing effectively with a specific example of your anxiety

Step 1: Describe the situation	
Step 2: Identify the unhealthy negative emotion in the situation (emotional 'C')	*Anxiety*
Step 3: How I act and think when I feel anxious (behavioural 'C' and thinking 'C')	
Step 4: What I am most anxious about in the situation ('A')	
Step 5: What is my rigid belief and main extreme belief at 'B' that accounts for my anxiety	
Step 6: Formulating alternative rational beliefs	

Step 7: Specifying goals (the healthy alternatives to anxiety and the behaviour and thinking that accompany it)	
Step 8: Questioning beliefs	
Step 9: Identifying behavioural and cognitive safety-seeking measures and their healthy alternatives	1 Behavioural safety-seeking measures and their healthy alternatives (in brackets): 2 Cognitive safety-seeking measures and their healthy alternatives (in brackets):
Step 10: Facing the specific threat in imagination while mentally rehearsing rational beliefs and acting and thinking accordingly	
Step 11: Facing the specific threat in reality while mentally rehearsing rational beliefs and acting and thinking accordingly	
Step 12: Coming back to 'A'	

Appendix 4: How Mike dealt with a specific example of his depression

Step 1: Describe the situation	*'The bid for the external contract that I headed up was not successful.'*
Step 2: Identify the unhealthy negative emotion in the situation (emotional 'C')	*Depression*
Step 3: How I act and think when I feel depressed (behavioural 'C' and thinking 'C')	*'I seriously thought about handing in my resignation and I went out to get very drunk.'*
Step 4: What I am most depressed about in the situation ('A')	*'I am most depressed about failing to do a good job on the bid.'*
Step 5: What is my rigid belief and main extreme belief at 'B' that accounts for my depression	*'I absolutely should have done a good job and the fact that I didn't proves that I am a failure.'*
Step 6: Formulating alternative rational beliefs	*'I wish I had done a good job, but I didn't have to do one. I am not a failure, I am a fallible human being who is capable of doing well and poorly.'*
Step 7: Specifying goals (the healthy alternatives to depression and the behaviour and thinking that accompany it)	*'I am aiming to feel sad, but not depressed, about not doing a good job on the bid and to think that I need to review my performance rather than resign. Instead of going out to get drunk, I can get feedback from my team and learn from what they have to say.'*

Step 8: Questioning beliefs	'I value doing well and wanted to do well on the bid, but that does not mean that I had to do well on it. If I had to do well, then I would have had to have done well. It is clear that there is no law of the universe that decrees that I have to do well. If there was, I could not go against it. I could literally not fail. Also, I am not a failure for failing to do well. My identity cannot be defined by my performance on the bid. I can prove that I am a fallible human being who is capable of doing well and poorly. If I were a failure then all I could do was fail and that is not the case.'
Step 9: Taking action and thinking in ways that are consistent with your rational beliefs	'Since it was important to me that I did well on the bid, I used my rational desire to review what had happened (subsequent thinking) instead of thinking about resigning, and to ask my team for feedback (behaviour) instead of getting drunk.'
Step 10: Coming back to 'A'	'While it is true that we did not win the bid, when I think about my performance objectively and from the feedback I got from my team, I can see now that while I made a few minor mistakes, I basically did do a good job on the bid. The general consensus among my team is that the company that won the bid did so because they had more money to spend on their bid than we did on ours.'

Appendix 5: 10 steps in dealing effectively with a specific example of your depression

Step 1: Describe the situation	
Step 2: Identify the problematic emotion in the situation (emotional 'C')	*Depression*
Step 3: How I act and think when I feel depressed (behavioural 'C' and thinking 'C')	
Step 4: What I am most depressed about in the situation ('A')	
Step 5: What is my rigid belief and main extreme belief at 'B' that accounts for my depression	
Step 6: Formulating alternative rational beliefs	

Step 7: Specifying goals (the healthy alternatives to depression and the behaviour and thinking that accompany it)	
Step 8: Questioning beliefs	
Step 9: Taking action and thinking in ways that are consistent with your rational beliefs	
Step 10: Coming back to 'A'	

Index

ABC framework, 7, 17–26, 58–64
    blank form, 231–2
    dealing with anxiety, 188–94,
        200–1
    dealing with depression, 215–18,
        224–5
    goal-based, 31–2, 44–7, 65–7
    identifying anxiety vs. concern,
        185–7
    identifying depression vs. sadness,
        207–8
    identifying vulnerability factors,
        146–7
    problem-based, 29–30, 42–4,
        200, 224
acceptance beliefs, 21–2, 33, 174
    vs. deprecation beliefs, 84–7
action tendency, 10, 11–12, 24, 25, 60
activity, physical, 214, 215
admitting to a problem, 29
adversity, 7, 18, 62–5, 129
    associated emotions, 35
    distortions of, 38
    exposure to, 97, 134–6, 157,
        193–4
    inferences held about, 38, 124–6
all-or-none thinking, 102–3, 107, 109
always-and-never thinking, 104, 107,
    112
anger, 8, 12, 14
anxiety, 8, 11, 35, 184–205
    example ABC form, 233–7
    identifying themes, 195–6
    as a meta-emotional problem,
        180
    public speaking, 18
    and self-control, 151–2
    specific example, 233–7
    vs. concern, 66, 185–7
assignments, self-help, 176–8
attack–response method, 90–2, 133–4
attribution, 115

autonomous depression, 210–12
    themes, 219
awfulizing beliefs, 19
    vs. non-awfulizing beliefs, 79–81

balanced thinking, 66–7
    vs. distorted inferences, 138
    vs. thinking errors, 106–16
Beck, Aaron T., 40
behaviour, 10–13
    associated emotions, 11–12
    and cognitive change, 168
    condoning, 172–3
    constructive, 10–11, 25, 134–6
    dysfunctional, 23–4, 60
    overcompensatory, 13, 167
    overt, 10, 23–4, 25, 60
    safety-seeking, 97, 168, 190–1,
        195–6
    self-protective, 12–13
    unconstructive, 10–11
behavioural consequences, 6, 10–12,
    60–1
    of irrational beliefs, 23–4
    of rational beliefs, 25
behavioural goals, 66
beliefs, 12–13, 18–22
    and conviction, 34, 96–7
    evaluation, 33, 73–87
    impact on behaviour, 10–11, 23–4
    impact on emotions, 7, 23
    rational vs. irrational, 2–6, 32–3
    see also core beliefs
blame, see attribution

change, barriers, 36–7, 159–61, 163–83
closure, 51–2
coaching, 95
commitment, 215
complacency, 174
concern, 8, 11
    vs. anxiety, 66, 185–7

condoning behaviour, *172–3*
confidence, *36–7, 198*
consequences, *6–7, 23–6, 58–62*
constructive behaviour, *10–11, 25, 134–6*
    imagery rehearsal, *148*
conviction, *34, 96–7*
    attack–response technique, *90–2, 133–4*
    coaching others, *95*
    rational-emotive imagery, *92–4, 147–8*
coping statements, *96, 157*
core beliefs, *130–8*
    and behavioural change, *222*
    questioning of, *132–3, 137–8*
    rational vs. irrational, *35–6*
    see also beliefs
counselling, *23*

denial, *167*
deprecation beliefs, *20*
    and depression, *209, 211*
    vs. acceptance beliefs, *33, 84–7*
depression, *8, 11, 35, 206–28*
    autonomous, *210–12, 219*
    example ABC form, *239–42*
    pity-related, *212–13, 220*
    routes into, *208–13, 219–20*
    sociotropic, *208, 209–10, 219*
    specific example, *239–42*
    vs. sadness, *67, 207–8*
development, personal, *155–61*
disappointment, *8, 11*
discomfort intolerance beliefs, *20*
    in depression, *209–10, 211*
    and psychological change, *179–80*
    vs. discomfort tolerance beliefs, *81–4*
discomfort tolerance beliefs, *21*
    and self-resignation, *173–4*
    vs. discomfort intolerance beliefs, *81–4*
dissatisfaction, *14, 15*
distorted thinking, *24, 38, 101–6*
    and adversity, *140–1, 201–3, 225–7*
    and thinking consequences, *136–40*
    and unhealthy negative emotions, *61–2*
    vs. balanced thinking, *197–8, 220–2*
    see also inferences
dysfunctional behaviour, *23–4, 60*

Ellis, Albert, *2, 156*
emotional consequences, *6, 7–9, 60*
    of irrational beliefs, *23*
    of rational beliefs, *25*
emotional disturbance, *14*
    admitting to a problem, *29*
emotional goals, *65*
emotional insight, *8–10, 89–90, 175*
emotional reasoning, *105, 107, 114*
emotions, *6–8*.
    associated behaviours, *11–12*
    meta-emotions, *180–1, 199–201, 223–5*
    see also healthy negative emotions; unhealthy negative emotions
envy, *8, 12, 35*
extreme beliefs, *19, 20, 68, 70*
    vs. non-extreme beliefs, *32*

failure, *35*
flexible beliefs, *20–1, 22*
    vs. rigid beliefs, *32, 69–70, 75–8*
fortune telling, *see* prediction

goals, *31–2, 40–7, 65–7*
    behavioural, *60*
    commitment to, *215*
    doubts about, *169–70*
    emotional, *65*
    formulation, *44–7*
    lapse and relapse, *143–53*
    list, *41–2*
    thinking, *66*
guilt, *8, 11*
    vs. remorse, *67*

healthy anger, *8, 67*
healthy envy, *8, 67*
healthy jealousy, *8, 67*

healthy negative emotions, 6–8
    associated behaviours, 11–12
    and balanced thinking, 66–7
    consequences of, 25–6
    in goal setting, 65–7
    vs. unhealthy negative emotions, 8, 25, 60
    see also emotions
hierarchy of needs, 15
homework, *see* assignments, self-help
hurt, 8, 12, 35
    vs. sorrow, 67

imagery rehearsal, 147–8, 150, 191–3
imagination, 92–4, 147–8, 191–13
in vivo exposure, 97, 134–6, 157, 193–4
inferences, 18, 124–6, 136–41
    consequential, 24, 101–2
    see also distorted thinking
inferential themes, 219–20
insight, 8–10, 89–90, 158–9, 174–5
intellectual insight, 8–10, 89, 158–9, 175
interpretation, *see* inferences
intolerance, *see* discomfort intolerance beliefs
irrational beliefs, 19–20
    about threats, 201–2
    awfulizing beliefs, 19, 79–81
    behavioural consequences, 10, 23
    core beliefs, 130–6
    deprecation beliefs, 20, 33, 84–7
    discomfort intolerance beliefs, 20, 81–4
    emotional consequences, 23, 60
    extreme beliefs, 19, 32, 68
    identification of, 68–9
    questioning of, 33, 157, 170
    rational alternatives, 32–3
    rigid beliefs, 19, 20, 32, 75–8
    thinking consequences, 24, 101–6, 116–21

jealousy, 8, 12, 35
jumping to conclusions, 102, 107, 108

lapses, 37, 144–50
laziness, 178
life events, *see* adversity
loss, 35

magnification, 104–5, 107, 113
Maslow, Abraham, 15
meta-emotional problems, 180–1
    anxiety, 199–201
    depression, 223–5
mind reading, 103–4, 107, 111
minimization, 105, 107, 113–14
    non-awfulizing beliefs, 172
motivation, 166, 171–2
multi-category thinking, 109

negative events, *see* adversity
negative focus, 103, 107, 109–10
non-awfulizing beliefs, 21, 69
    and condoning behaviour, 172–3
    vs. awfulizing beliefs, 79–81
non-extreme beliefs, 20–2, 32, 69, 70

other people, 165–6
overcompensation, 13, 167
overgeneralization, 103, 107, 109
overt behaviour, 10, 23–4, 25, 60

past experience, 164–5
perfectionism, 135
personal development, 14–15, 155–61
personal domain, 185
personalization, 105, 107, 114–15
perspective, 113, 114
physical activity, 214, 215
pity-related depression, 212–13
    themes, 220
positive disqualification, 103, 107, 110
prediction, 104, 107, 111–12
problem list, 40–2, 44–7
    prioritizing problems, 49–51
    target problem, 49–55
progress, 155–61
public speaking, 18

rational beliefs, *2–6, 20–2*
  acceptance beliefs, *69, 84–7*
  behavioural consequences, *10, 25*
  and constructive behaviour, *11*
  core beliefs, *131–6*
  discomfort tolerance beliefs,
    21, 69, 81–4
  emotional consequences, *25, 60*
  flexible beliefs, *20–1, 22, 32,*
    69–71, 75–8
  identification of, *69–71*
  non-awfulizing beliefs, *21, 69,*
    79–81
  non-extreme beliefs, *21–2, 32,*
    69, 70
  thinking consequences, *26*
  unconditional acceptance beliefs,
    21–2, 33
  vs. irrational beliefs, *32–3, 69–71,*
    93–4
rational-emotive imagery, *92–4,*
  147–8, 149–50
rehearsing, *see* imagery rehearsal
relapse, *37, 143–4, 150–3*
relationships, *209–10*
remorse, *11*
  vs. guilt, *67*
resignation, *174*
responsibility, *163–4*
  for progress, *155–6*
rigid beliefs, *19, 20, 32, 68, 70*
  vs. flexible beliefs, *75–8*

sadness, *8, 11*
  vs. depression, *207–8*
safety-seeking behaviour, *97, 168,*
  190–1, 195–7
self-acceptance, *see* acceptance beliefs
self-actualization, *15*
self-care, *209–10*
self-compassion, *222–3*
self-control, *151–2*
self-deprecation, *see* deprecation beliefs
self-help, *176–8*
self-pity, *212–13*
self-resignation, *174*

self-statements, *see* coping statements
shame, *11, 35*
short-term solutions, *166*
situational analysis, *see* ABC
  framework
sociotropic depression, *208, 209–10*
  themes, *219*
sorrow, *8, 12*
  vs. hurt, *67*

talking it over, *214*
target problem, *49–55*
therapy, stages, *13–15, 29–38*
thinking consequences, *6, 100–8*
  and distorted thinking, *136–40*
  of irrational beliefs, *24, 101–6,*
    116–21
  of rational beliefs, *25*
thinking errors, *102–6, 108–16*
thinking goals, *66*
threat, *35, 184–7*
  and distorted thinking, *201–4*
  exposure, *191–4, 199*
time commitments, *177–8*
tolerance, *see* discomfort tolerance
  beliefs

uncertainty, *141, 202–3, 225–7*
unconditional acceptance beliefs, *21–2*
unconstructive behaviour, *10*
understanding, *see* insight
unhealthy anger, *8, 12, 14, 35*
unhealthy envy, *8, 12, 35*
unhealthy jealousy, *8, 12, 35*
unhealthy negative emotions, *6–8, 23,*
  58–60
  and adversity, *35*
  associated behaviours, *11–12*
  and distorted thinking, *61–2*
  healthy alternatives, *8, 25, 93–4,*
    157–8
  see also emotions

visualization, *see* imagery rehearsal;
  rational-emotive imagery
vulnerability, *37, 145–50*